# When Christians FAIL

D1555820

# When Christians FAIL

### Finding a Way Forward

**Michael Apichella**

**MARC**

**British Library Cataloguing in Publication Data**

Apichella, Michael
   When Christians fail.
   1. Failure (Christian theology)
   I. Title
   248.4     BT730.5

   ISBN 0–947697–79–9

Unless otherwise noted, Scripture quotations in this publication are taken from *The Living Bible,* copyright © 1971 by Tyndale House Publishers, Wheaton, IL. Used by permission.

# Contents

In Memory of
Dominic 'Deek' DeCusatis,
my dear friend,
whose death coincided with the writing of this book;
and to my wife and friend, Judith,
who suggested I write about failure.

I wish to express my gratitude to the following: the Revd PH Rogers of Oxford for his constructive criticism and fatherly encouragement; to my editor, Karen Barnes, whose hard work and marathon editing session in London helped to make this book a reality; and to Craig and Robin Hill—who more than once came to our rescue in 100 practical ways, most recently when our daughter, Elizabeth Rose, was born 3 weeks early while I was in the midst of finishing this book. Thanks!

Special thanks to William Collins, Sons & Company, Ltd for permission to quote CS Lewis' 'Pilgrim's Problem' and portions of *The Great Divorce*, and also to Methodist Publishing House for their kind consent to reprint John Wesley's Covenant.

# Introduction

Be honest. Have you ever been angry because you felt abandoned by God when you seemed to need him most? Do you get depressed because others seem to succeed while you just muddle along? Perhaps there are times when you contemplate committing suicide because you feel you've 'made a mess of your life'? If so, then this book may be for you. This book is about the anger, the pain and the suffering which comes about when Christians fail.

For better or worse, we've been conditioned to judge ourselves and others by certain achievements. And when our achievements don't match up to our expectations, this serves to fuel the destructive force of failure. While it is perfectly natural that we compare ourselves to others, one of Satan's favourite ploys is to make us feel dissatisfied with ourselves and ultimately with God. In his book, *Confessions of a Parish Priest*, Andrew M Greeley questions this common practice:

> Several Catholic critics, especially a woman who writes regularly for *Commonweal* ... and who makes kind of a career of attacking me, cheerfully announce to their readers that I am not Greene or Waugh or Mauriac or Undset or Michelangelo or Dante. Such comments are supposed to devastate me and warn off readers.
>
> Well, patently, I am not any of those folk. Moreover, I am not James Joyce, Agatha Christie, Marcel Proust or Flann O'Brien either.... But so what? Why need I be any of these people? And more to the point, why should my

work be evaluated against theirs? … Why isn't it
enough to be me?[1]

Likewise, when Paul was unfavourably compared
to other more popular preachers of his day, his only
reply was, 'Their trouble is that they are only comparing themselves with each other…. Our goal is to measure up to God's plan for us' (II Cor 10:12–13).

Greeley and Paul are saying that our intrinsic value
lies in the fact that God calls us to be his children—he
loves us, and we are formed in his image. Even if
others—or we ourselves—think we are dismal failures, we are infinitely valuable and are wholly accept-
able in God's eyes. Of course, knowing this hardly
relieves the anguish we feel, but it should keep things
in perspective when our best attempts fall short of the
mark.

Look at the great men and women of faith in the
Bible. How many escaped the bracing slaps of defeat
as they tried to live their lives for God and his kingdom? When Moses and the Jews marched trium-
phantly out of bondage in Egypt, leaving an awe-
struck Pharaoh in their wake, or when the zealous
apostle Peter amazed his friends by venturing out on
to the Sea of Galilee on foot—both these men of God
were pressing towards the stony precipice of defeat.
Mercifully, God preserved a written record to remind
us that very few saints get through this life unscathed.
At least *our* failures aren't immortalised in a gold-
leaf, leather-bound best seller like the Bible, for all
generations to see.

Knowing that biblical saints have failed is sometimes only a small compensation and does very little to
restore our equilibrium when our own best-laid plans
turn sour. To fail is a serious blow to a Christian's
faith. When it happens, we feel cheated, hurt and

angry. However, self-pity is a dangerous and vulnerable emotion. Satan, who understands failure only too well as a result of his own fall from grace (see Rev 12:7–9), is ever busy whispering his deadly lies in our ears. His delight is to push God's chosen people to the brink, as he did with Judas Iscariot and King Saul, both of whom failed while serving God, but then succumbed to morbid introspection, despair and finally suicide.

If these chapters do anything, may they be an encouragement to Christians who must endure the stinging-nettles of life—whether through a broken marriage, humiliation at work, failed health, a fruitless ministry, or any of a hundred other possible heartbreaks. These are painful and lonely experiences, but our failures needn't destroy us. We only have to look at the lives of men and women in the Bible for evidence that '… all that happens to us is working for our good if we love God and are fitting into his plans' (Rom 8:28). Lest you think I am citing this particular passage as some sort of panacea which will protect us from the withering realities of sin, fallen human nature and bitter failure, I am aware of cases which, humanly speaking, are hopeless and without apparent resolve. I know missionaries who, certain of God's calling to the field, have returned home in ignoble defeat, like shattered china dolls. Instead of coming home for a triumphant furlough to spend time with friends and family, they are quietly relegated to mental hospitals, some for as long as 10 years, without showing any sign of recovery. I am also aware of tragic cases where people are suffering through debilitating illnesses. As a result, these people feel they are failing both themselves and their families—while constantly questioning God, wondering desperately why healing does not come. I cannot hope to offer solutions to

problems such as these—indeed, I do not feel qualified to do so. Rather, this book aims to cast some
illumination on our failings, giving pointers towards a
deeper understanding of the overall problem.

Contrary to the popular myth that Christians
should always expect unmitigated success in their
lives, the truth is, Christians can and do fail. In this
book I describe four basic reasons why I believe God
allows us to fail: sometimes the Lord allows failure as
a means of bringing about a greater good; in other instances, failure keeps us from becoming too puffed up
with our accomplishments; still another reason is unconfessed, volitional sin; and finally, there are times
when Christians fail simply because, as with all human
beings, they make a bad decision or are overcome by a
natural disaster.

Although the two are closely linked, this book is
about failure, not suffering. In every case, what I have
to say is applicable to individual, not corporate failure. Therefore, I do not attempt to deal with such
topics as the starving people nor the abject poverty of
the underdeveloped nations of the world.

I do not pretend to explain every reason why God
allows Christians to experience failure. No one may
claim to do that. It is a futile exercise to manipulate
events to fit in with our own limited understanding of
the Almighty. When we try to assess God through our
limited human understanding, as Job tried to do,
God's awesome response is, 'Why are you using your
ignorance to deny my providence? ... Where were you
when I laid the foundations of the earth? Tell me, if
you know so much (Job 38:2–4). Clearly, the Christian faith revolves around the unseen—and when it
comes down to it, we have to give over to God the
many things beyond our comprehension, just as the
men and women of the Bible did.

Finally, this book seeks to be a resource tool for those who want to support and encourage others through times of despair. From my own experience of failure, at the *time* there is a strong tendency to reject the encouragement of the written word. At such black moments, upholding and undergirding from other Christians are invaluable and often help us to catch hold of the anchor for which we so desperately reach. God is that anchor.

## Notes

[1] Andrew M Greeley, *Confessions of a Parish Priest* (Simon & Schuster: New York, 1986), pp 46–47.

# Chapter 1

# Success At Any Price?

### The Great Swindle?

Oh, the joys of those who do not follow evil men's advice, who do not hang around with sinners, scoffing at the things of God: but they delight in doing everything God wants them to, and day and night are always meditating on his laws and thinking about ways to follow him more closely. They are like trees along a river-bank bearing luscious fruit each season without fail. Their leaves shall never wither, and all they do shall prosper. (Psalm 1:1–3)

If we understand the psalmist's simile correctly, failure is a thing reserved for the wicked, the scheming, the morally bankrupt and other assorted baddies. When we become Christians, surely our lives should be exempt from embarrassing failures and heart-breaking disappointments? Thus we sing with confidence,

> O may this bounteous God
> Through all our life be near us,
> With ever joyful hearts
> And blessèd peace to cheer us;
> And keep us in his grace,
> And guide us when perplexed,
> And free us from all ills
> In this world and the next.[1]

For many of us, these comforting words are an encouragement. But what happens when Christians set about serving God in earnest, only to have their plans go wrong? What effect does this upset have on believers who are defeated by overwhelming circumstances? Is the psalmist lying when he promises that God will not allow his children to fail? Are the words of the hymnal nothing more than wishful thinking grounded on a delusion?

A few years ago, a young, energetic Presbyterian minister, David Armstrong, extended his church's outreach into Belfast's Magilligan Prison, where convicted Irish terrorists are housed in three H-Blocks. It became apparent to Armstrong that his calling in Ulster was to bring reconciliation to warring Protestants and Roman Catholics.

Finding himself in a community not noted for its religious tolerance, the Presbyterian minister decided his only hope of successfully breaking down centuries old walls of fear was to rely on the power of the gospel of Christ. In his book *A Road Too Wide*, Armstrong writes about his early attempts at reconciliation: 'I believed that if people seriously consider the claims of Jesus and look at his character as revealed in the New Testament, then his love for them shown in his death on the Cross can be a transforming power.'[2] Ironically, instead of being transformed by the power of the Cross, he found people hardened by the power of fear. Many Protestants condemned his attempts at finding common ground with the Roman Catholics, and Armstrong became the target of an ugly smear campaign. Even some close associates in his church refused to side with their leader after Armstrong befriended a neighbouring Roman Catholic priest whose church had been bombed in a night raid by terrorists. His continued efforts to foster forgiveness and reconciliation brought his family cruel threats of physical abuse, isolation and betrayal.

Armstrong noticed, too, that his actions were having a negative effect not only in his church and on his family life, but in the community at large. At more than one church service where Armstrong was helping officiate, demonstrators began heckling him and disrupting the proceedings. Rather than pulling the Roman Catholic and Protestant factions together, Armstrong appeared to be fuelling the fires of hatred that divided the two denominations. It must be said that many of his fellow Christians privately sided with him, but Armstrong admits, 'I was beginning to realise that ... I would not be able to stay [in my church] much longer if I did not have the support of my elders.'[3]

In the end Armstrong had to concede defeat: after two years of wrestling with hopelessness, for the sake of peace, he left Ulster, abandoning the work he had begun, his congregation and even the Presbyterian Church of Ireland. He carried with him to England the brutal scars of a profound failure. What happened to God's promise that those who seek ways to follow him more closely and serve him are 'like trees along a river bank bearing luscious fruit each season without fail'? Could it be that Armstrong was deluded?

His is not the only example of a Christian who failed. An Oxford don, CS Lewis, set about presenting the case for Christianity through such books as *Mere Christianity*, *The Problem of Pain*, and *Miracles*. He was dubbed 'The Apostle to the Sceptics' by *Time* magazine because he managed to present intellectual arguments for faith that appealed to agnostics—something other twentieth-century apologists had failed to do successfully.

In 1951, after 27 years of teaching at the University, Lewis was snubbed by his colleagues when passed over for a much deserved promotion to full professor.

His elder brother, Warren, recorded in his diary on Thursday, February 8th, 1951, 'I confess I'm astonished at the virulence of the anti-Xian [Christian] feeling shown here.'[4] Warren Lewis went on to state that many fellows and dons had voted against his brother simply because he had written popular Christian books.

Eventually, Lewis had to resign from Oxford in order to have a promotion. In 1954 he became professor of Medieval and Renaissance Literature at Cambridge University. Sadly, this honour was short-lived, for by 1960 he was critically ill and within two years had to resign owing to failing health.

God promises to bless us when we serve him, so when we have little or no fruit to show for our labour—only scars—his promise can irritate like a cinder in the eye, and all the joy of being a Christian can go out of the window. Are God's promises nothing more than an *incredible* deception? Why must Christians such as Armstrong and Lewis fail? It must be admitted that there is no easy answer to the question.

## A Popular Misconception

Theologian Leslie D Weatherhead claims that regardless of how we perceive a situation, nothing has the power to defeat us or God.

> One thing *is* incredible.... That God should allow circumstances [to happen] which inevitably defeat his ultimate purposes. If he did, it would mean that he abdicated from the throne of the universe, whereas the truth is that, though the [situation] ... seems formidable, 'the Lord God omnipotent reigneth.'[5]

What does this mean to Christians? First, the popular belief that Christians will always be successful, at least in material terms, is a misconception. It must be said that becoming a Christian is not like taking out a powerful insurance that for ever spares the signatory the pain of failure. Next, if we read Psalm 1 only, we are guilty of gross ignorance. The key to understanding what happens when Christians fail is better understood in another psalm:

> He does not fear bad news, nor live in dread of
> what may happen. For he is settled in his mind
> that Jehovah will take care of him. That is why
> he is not afraid, but can calmly face his foes.
>                               (Psalm 112:7–8)

These words, taken with Psalm 1, give us the fuller understanding of God's promise to bless and protect his followers: God is not deceiving us when we do fail, he is actually busy fulfilling his promise of ultimate success to Christians even when they *appear* to fail. Unfortunately, few of us are willing to accept this fact.

Today appearances are terribly important. For example, I have seen Christian books that teach the reader how to dress for success. Some promise that we will win friends and influence people only when we look our best! Of course it is good to look smart, but we must not allow outward appearances, success, and status symbols to be our touchstone.

Several years ago, I worked at the reception desk of The American Church of Paris. This is a large, affluent church. One Sunday an African man appeared at the desk, asking to see the pastor. I looked at the worn cuffs of his shirt and his old-fashioned suit and began to fob him off, saying that the pastor was busy. After the man had walked out to the street, the words of James came crashing down on my head like a cold Atlantic breaker, 'Dear brothers, how can you claim that you belong to the Lord Jesus Christ, the Lord of Glory, if you show favouritism to rich people and look down on poor people?' (James 2:1). I leaped over the barrier and scrambled down the steps which led to Quai D'Orsay, hoping to find the man I had just rejected solely on his appearance. Sadly, he was nowhere in sight. Later on, I noted in my journal that I had turned Christ out of his church: 'When you refused to help the least of these my brothers, you were refusing to help me' (Matt 25:45).

## Win At All Costs

We live in a society that believes winning isn't everything; it's the *only* thing. Of course failure is hard to swallow. Dread of individual failure has become for our culture what the dread of individual sin had been for our ancestors. Pagans in the last century said of the Victorians, 'Being European means they must sin in private.' I think it may be said of modern Europe and the United States, 'Being Westerners, they must fail in private.' Put another way, our culture views failure as vice and success as virtue.

It is worthwhile to consider what has happened in Germany. The young tennis professional Boris Becker was quoted as saying of his recent tennis victories, 'The Germans wanted me to live for them. They worshipped too much. When I entered my home town people stood there and gazed up at me as if they were expecting blessings from the Pope.'[6] One wonders how his compatriots might have received him had Becker not beaten the world's number-One-ranked tennis player, Ivan Lendl, at Wimbledon. Boris Becker is young to have such great expectations heaped on his back. Fortunately, he is still able to say of himself, 'I'm still beatable. I'm human.'[7] Christians should remember that they are human, too.

Germany is not alone in this cult-like worship of winning: it is a problem common to all humanity. The abhorrence of failure is endemic, worming its way even into the Church. Significantly, Tony Cummings, writing in *Buzz Magazine*, claims that the Church is guilty of massive accommodation to worldly standards. Cummings claims that, long ago, the Church invaded the world. Today the world has invaded the Church.[8] If Christians are influenced by this worldly idea of 'win at all costs', then it is no wonder we question God's veracity when we fail. Failure disrupts our equilibrium and rocks our faith in God's goodness.

Moreover, Cummings argues that Christians have become addicted to comfort and ease to a dangerous degree:

> Possibly the most pervasive and easily identifiable manifestation of worldliness is materialism.... That if I honour God, he will bless me with material prosperity. That if I serve, I have the right to expect that my house and car will get bigger and my bank balance will get fatter[9]

To a watchful and—may I say emphatically—a sceptical world outside the Church, it is obvious there is something 'not on' within the Church when many of the leaders and members of the congregation live in relative comfort and ease, while the founder of the faith says, 'Remember, I don't even own a place to lay my head. Foxes have dens to live in, and birds have nests, but I, the Messiah, have no earthly home at all' (Luke 9:58).

## No Pain—No Gain

The pain of failure is a reality for Christians. Although we would rather not face our faults, we must come to terms with the unpleasant side of following Christ. For the sake of argument, let's assume that a fair amount of failure is a necessary part of Christian experience. All parents know their children are destined to fail from time to time. They also know that, following each mistake, there comes the dawning of the great 'aha'—that moment when the light dawns and a puzzle is solved. Occasional failure allows children to learn from experience, to develop critical skills which later allow them to cope with similar problems and achieve their fullest potential. Although it may be quite painful, failure is an excellent teacher.

The Bible presents God as a parent. If God is a good father, then we may assume that from his point of view failure may actually bring about success in the long run. 'Let God train you,' says the writer of Hebrews, 'for he is doing what any loving father does for his children. Whoever heard of a son [or daughter] who was never corrected?' (Hebrews 12:7).

If we doubt that any good may come about as the result of experiences which are utterly humiliating and painful, let's consider CS Lewis once more.

Of course Lewis was not a total failure. At Oxford he had earned a reputation for being a pugnacious debater who hated to lose: and his close circle of friends, including JRR Tolkien and the novelist Charles Williams, considered his to be one of the finest minds in the University. Moreover, Lewis himself admitted his own struggle with a superiority complex and latent priggishness. Remaining as a lowly don for the best part of his academic career, while his friends eased into the choice senior academic posts, had kept this vastly gifted man humble—therefore he bore the indelible stamp of Christ. It is no wonder his books continue to influence millions of readers around the world today.

But don't think that Lewis was not grieved by the unfair treatment he received at Oxford. Bitter disappointment, but not despair, is evident in his poem 'Pilgrim's Problem'. Note the end:

By now I should be entering on the supreme stage
Of the whole walk, reserved for the late afternoon.
The heat was to be over now; the anxious mountains,
The airless valleys and the sun-baked rocks behind me.
Now, or soon now, if all is well, come the majestic
Rivers of foamless charity that glide beneath
Forests of contemplation. In the grassy clearings
Humility with liquid eyes and damp, cool nose
Should come, half tame, to eat bread from my hermit hand.
If storms arose, then in my tower of fortitude—
It ought to have been in sight by this—I would take refuge;
But I expected rather a pale mackerel sky,
Feather-like, perhaps shaking from a lower cloud
Light drops of silver temperance, and cloverly earth
Sending up mists of chastity, a country smell,
Till earnest stars blaze out in the established sky
Rigid with justice; the streams audible; my rest secure.
I can see nothing like this. Was the map wrong?
Maps can be wrong. But the experienced walker knows
That the other explanation is more often true.[10]

While he was unhappy, Lewis the pilgrim decided to accept his circumstances, trusting God who, after all, is the master map-maker.

Paul, also a highly gifted man, comments that God purposely kept him humble through something referred to cryptically as his 'thorn in the flesh' (II Cor 12:7). What's more, even though Paul knew it was—

for better or worse—painfully necessary that he suffer, he asked God to free him of the stigma. I take heart from the fact that Paul did not decide to accept his lot stoically. Had he not complained, it would be hard for me to see him as human. I do not like failure or pain much, either.

> I was given a physical condition which has been a thorn in my flesh, a messenger from Satan to hurt and bother me, and prick my pride. Three different times I begged God to make me well again.
> Each time he said, 'No. But I am with you; that is all you need. My power shows up best in weak people.'
>
> (II Cor 12:7–9)

Paul's prayers failed to change his discomfort with the result that God was able to use him in establishing the Early Church.

## Irony

Are we to infer, then, that the only reason why God allows Christians to suffer failure is to keep them humble? Hardly. Let's turn back to David Armstrong's case. Unlike Lewis or Paul, he did not have all the advantages of a first-rate education. Neither was his a comfortable, upper-class home-life as a child. Armstrong's father was a butcher, and Armstrong himself was employed in a routine job with the Northern Ireland Electricity Board when he felt the call to enter the ministry. He had few 'O' levels and no 'A' levels, let alone a command of Greek and Latin! His humbling experience was to return to the classroom as an adult. In addition, throughout his formal education, Armstrong had to work harder than his classmates because he was married and the father of three children. It is unlikely that God allowed Armstrong's ministry to fail in order to keep him humble! So why did God allow the Armstrongs to suffer so searing a failure? A brief analysis of the aftermath of the events may shed some light on God's reasons.

In an interview appearing in the *Northern Constitution* on May 4th, 1985, Armstrong reflected sadly, 'This past year has not been easy for me … it took a lot out of me…. I feel I have not achieved all I thought I might have.' He added, 'I realise I am full of shortcomings and failures.'[11]

By all appearances, Armstrong's valiant efforts to bring Christian harmony to a small town in Northern Ireland have failed. Yet viewed from another angle, his tragic set-back has been picked up by the news media, and currently his failure is doing more to cause widespread unity among Roman Catholics and Ulster Protestants than if his former ministry had succeeded quietly. In his book, *A Road Too Wide*, Armstrong writes—as a result of the incidents which led up to his seeming defeat—'Eighteen leaders of the Irish Presbyterian Church had sent a signed letter to the press, saying that they supported what I had done, and were working for reconciliation in their churches.'[12] The Armstrongs are still not over their pain, and the fear they felt still lurks in the background. Admittedly, the problems in Ulster are far from resolved. Yet a letter from a Northern Ireland church magazine commenting on David's bad experiences is evidence that his failure was necessary in bringing about his dream of reconciliation between Protestants and Roman Catholics in Ulster:

Did we try to do anything about it? Did we write

him [Armstrong] a letter of support? Did we write to our assembly, supporting this (reconciliation) work? Did we write to our ministers, insisting they try to do something—or to our session?

No! We have lost a man who felt isolated, saddened and dismayed because some people felt he was a threat to their religion!

There is only one David Armstrong, one David Armstrong...' or maybe there are more. LET'S MAKE SURE WE DON'T LOSE THE NEXT ONE.

Thank you, David. Take care.[13]

## The Swindle?

Here, then, are two reasons why God allows Christians to fail. The first is to keep us humble and dependent on God; the second is to bring about victory—though not perhaps in the way we had expected. Later we will examine other reasons why Christians fail. As I said earlier, the Bible gives many examples of men and women who have set out to serve God, but who failed either as a result of making errors, sinning, or just facing overwhelming circumstances—Saul, David, Judas Iscariot, and Mark among them.

Looking at the lives of these people who each knew serious failures will help us to understand why God allows us to fail, and how he is able to use our shortcomings to bring about his ultimate successes. Paul is therefore sincere when, after enduring public ridicule, floggings, prison sentences and harsh censure from his fellow Christians, he writes:

Since I know it is all for Christ's good, I am quite happy about 'the thorn,' and about insults and hardships, persecutions and difficulties; for

when I am weak, then I am strong—the less I
have, the more I depend on him.

(II Cor 12:10)

Are we then to conclude that the promise of per-
petual success made in Psalm 1 is nothing more than a
swindle, since it is clear to all that Christians do experience failure and the suffering associated with it?
Hardly. But there is one who would like us to turn on
God and curse his name when we fail. It is this one
who is the true swindler. The Devil wants us to believe
that God doesn't care about the hurts we suffer while
serving him. And like all great swindles, Satan's lie is
simple ... and deadly.

## Notes

[1]*Hymns Ancient & Modern Revised* (William Clowes
& Sons, Ltd: London) p 300.

[2]David Armstrong, *A Road Too Wide* (Marshall Pickering: Basingstoke, 1985), p 91.

[3]*ibid* p 140.

[4]Clyde S Kilby and Marjorie Lamp Mead (eds),
*Brothers and Friends* (Harper & Row Publishers:
Cambridge, Mass, 1982), pp 239–40.

[5]Leslie D Weatherhead, *The Will of God* (Abingdon
Press: Nashville, 1972), pp 29–30.

[6]Pico Lyer, 'Hero in a Land of Few Heroes', *Time*
(June 30th, 1986): p 14.

[7]Sara C Medina, 'People', *Time* (July 21st, 1986): p 21.

[8]Tony Cummings, 'How the Church was Lost', *Buzz
Magazine* (June 1985): pp 28–30.

[9]*ibid* p 29.

[10]Walter Hooper (ed), *CS Lewis Poems* (Geoffrey
Bles: London, 1966), p 119. (Permission to use 'Pil-
grim's Problem' by courtesy of William Collins, Sons
& Co Ltd.)

[11]'Many Visibly Moved As Revd David Armstrong Says Goodbye,' *Northern Constitution* (May 4th, 1985).
[12]Armstrong, *op cit*, p 155.
[13]*ibid* p 159.

# Chapter 2
# As A Father Would To His Son

In 1982, 6 years after leaving university, I was a tenured teacher at a school in Cecil County, Maryland. I had most of the perks one could ask for: paid sick leave, lots of holidays, a good pension scheme and a comprehensive life insurance plan—to name but a few. To most people, I probably appeared to be a very successful man—and in many ways, I was. I loved my wife. I enjoyed teaching. I belonged to a good church. But deep within me I was actually frustrated; I felt my true vocation was to be a journalist, not a teacher.

During one of our many walks in the wilderness of Turkey Point on the north shore of the Chesapeake Bay, my wife and I discussed my leaving teaching and returning to college to work on a Masters Degree in journalism. 'If you're sure that this is God's will,' Judith said cautiously, 'then I support the idea 100 per cent.'

'I can't be *sure* it's God's will—who can ever be certain of that?' I retorted as I watched the silver-flecked tide lap against the toes of my Wellington boots. I picked up a stick and flung it out on to the murky water. After a long pause, I added, 'I think I could serve God better as a journalist than as a teacher.' Then I bit down on my lower lip and continued, 'I want to serve God first, you see—only I'm too afraid to actually do it.'

Judith was quiet. Turning to face her, I pointed out, 'You know, if we decide to make the change, we'll have to give up all that we have now—our jobs, our friends, our security, everything we've ever worked for—and begin all over again, knowing in the end there is no certainty that I'll ever find a job as a journalist. Are you willing to do that?'

'I tell you what,' Judith said, 'you just make applications now, and when the time comes, I'll go along with whatever you decide.'

Later that year I was accepted at a college in the Midwest—a thousand miles inland. Now the question was no longer hypothetical. For years, we'd counselled others to trust God completely; suddenly we knew it was our chance to put what we believed into practice.

After I cashed my final pay-cheque for the term, I walked down to the bay to pray that God would guide us as we made this hard decision. As I sat on the twisted trunk of an uprooted oak tree with my bare feet buried snugly in the cool sand, I spotted a tiny sail-boat with two people manning it. I watched it move away from the dockyard where all the other boats were safely moored. As the two-man crew tacked into the fickle winds—sometimes making good headway, sometimes threatening to draw to a halt as they pressed towards the unseen shore in the distance —it seemed a perfect metaphor for our setting out to find God's will: we must have faith in ourselves and in the unseen hand of God, even when the odds are against us. Suddenly I knew what I had to do.

That evening, I wrote a letter of resignation from my teaching post and felt overcome by the fear and excitement of knowing an irreversible decision to trust God for our security had been made. In less than three months, Judith and I would be trusting God for our financial well-being.

To raise money for our trip west, we sold off most of

our household items—furniture, books, appliances—
keeping only the essentials. The rest we gave away.

After much thought, we decided to use part of our
savings to pay for the first year of college rather than
to apply for an education loan as most American students must. 'After all,' said Judith, 'you're still paying
off your first college loan. If you add another 10,000
dollars to that, we'll be in debt for the rest of our
lives.' After saying our last farewells to friends and
family in the east, we then hired a small trailer to hold
our worldly goods, and set off for Chicago in my
beaten-up Volkswagen 'beetle'.

That first year we lived in a small bed-sit. We had no
telephone, our shared bathroom was down the hall,
and we cooked all of our meals on a portable, one-ring
stove. Eventually, we both found jobs. Judith worked
as a receptionist for a publisher and I worked part
time in the sales department. Because of the odd
hours I worked in the day, I often sat up late with a
pillowcase over the lamp, studying while Judith slept.
She didn't mind the light so much as the noise of my
little electric typewriter as I pecked away into the
night, writing essays, stories and reports. All through
that first year we found ourselves just scraping by.
Our biggest worry, though, was finding enough
money to complete the second year of my studies.

At the end of the first year, the college offered a
special grant to students whose savings and income
were below a certain level. We qualified for the grant
in all respects but one: we had 500 dollars in the bank
which was given to us as a wedding present. We had
agreed to use the money only in an emergency. However, the gift made us ineligible for the grant by about
200 dollars.

Without telling my wife, I applied for the grant anyway, but lied about the true amount of my savings.

'God wants me to finish my degree,' I rationalised as I signed the forms. 'Otherwise he'd never have led us out here in the first place.'

Although on paper I appeared to qualify for the money, for some reason my application was rejected. After an initial period of disappointment, I buried myself in my work, forgetting about the lie I had told. But soon a series of bad events began to unfold.

Some friends invited my wife and me to a picnic in a park. While playing baseball, an accident left me with two broken fingers on my left hand. The pain of the fractures was insignificant compared to the pain of paying the bill for the medical treatment at hospital. Even with insurance, we had to pay 100 dollars. Since there is no National Health Service in the USA, the money had to come from our savings.

Just before the start of the new term, the college announced an increase in fees that meant we had to create a new budget if I was to finish the course I had begun. Subsequently, Judith and I took odd jobs at the weekends such as baby-sitting, warehouse work and house-sitting to help defray the mounting costs of my education.

There was one bright spot, though—my sales turnover had always been high, so we were never totally broke. But suddenly and quite inexplicably, my sales averages dropped lower and lower until I considered myself almost a liability to the company. Although the women I worked with were setting monthly records for high sales, it seemed I couldn't even *give* away our products. As my take-home pay diminished week after week, we moved rapidly from tightening our belts to almost being on the breadline. In the end, we were using the remnant of our savings just to live.

The final blow came when our elderly landlady gave us notice that we would have to move because her grandson needed a place to live—she was offering him our room. Judith and I knew we could not afford any more. In desperation, we turned to God and cried, 'Why are you allowing this to happen to us, Lord?'

### Sin

When Christians sin of their own volition, God needs to remind them of his total hatred of sin. In the Old Testament, failure comes to Joshua, a man ordained by God to lead the chosen people into the Promised Land. He fails because some men in his camp have wilfully sinned against God's holy law. A brilliant military campaign ends in ignoble failure when the Israelites are defeated while trying to capture the small city of Ai, east of Bethel:

> Joshua cried out to the Lord, 'O Jehovah, why have you brought us over the Jordan River if you are going to let the Amorites kill us?...'
> But the Lord said to Joshua, 'Get up off your face! Israel has sinned and disobeyed my commandment and has taken loot when I said it was not to be taken; and they have not only taken it, they have lied about it and have hidden it among their belongings. That is why the people of Israel are being defeated. That is why your men are running from their enemies—for they are cursed. I will not stay with you any longer unless you completely rid yourselves of this sin.'
>
> (Josh 7:7, 10–12)

It is wilful disobedience that incurs God's wrath and causes Joshua to fail. Bear in mind what I said in Chapter 1 regarding failure—there are many reasons why people fail. Unconfessed sin in our lives is but one.

When Christians intentionally sin, God's action

needs to be swift and final, or else they will be doomed
to endure more failure—even though they are on a
mission ordained by God himself. Let's look at King
David, one referred to by God as 'a man after [my] …
own heart' (I Sam 13:14 [RSV]). After becoming in-
fatuated with Bathsheba, David arranges to sleep
with her even though he knows it is wrong. That night
he makes her pregnant. To try to cover up his sin,
David orders the death of her husband, Uriah, one of
his loyal officers. Thinking he has covered his tracks,
David then takes Bathsheba as his own wife and hopes
the whole sordid affair will never come to light. But
the prophet Nathan comes to David and says:

> 'Why, then, have you despised the laws of God
> and done this horrible deed? For you have mur-
> dered Uriah and stolen his wife. Therefore mur-
> der shall be a constant threat in your family
> from this time on, because you have insulted me
> by taking Uriah's wife. I vow [says the Lord]
> that because of what you have done I will cause
> your own household to rebel against you. I will
> give your wives to another man, and he will go
> to bed with them in public view. You did it sec-
> retly, but I will do this to you openly, in the sight
> of all Israel.'
>
> (II Sam 12:9–12)

In the New Testament, Ananias is the hypocrite
who sells his property, but holds back a portion of the
money with the assistance of his wife, Sapphira,
though both claim they have given the full value to the
church. Peter sharply rebukes Ananias, saying,
'Ananias, Satan has filled your heart. When you
claimed this was the full price, you were lying to the
Holy Spirit' (Acts 5:3). Peter points out that nobody
forced Ananias to sell his property—it was something

he decided to do of his own free will. 'How could you do a thing like this?' demands Peter. 'You weren't lying to us, but to God' (Acts 5:4). At these words, Ananias drops dead—I wouldn't care to speculate about the cause of his death.

If they do anything, these three passages suggest that God is sometimes willing to send failure into people's lives as a means of chastising them for their unconfessed volitional sins. What's more, the passages tell us something about the nature of the Christian's relationship with God, for God won't tolerate premeditated sinning among people who have entered into a relationship with him, trusting God as their saviour and giving consent that he may come into their lives and take control.

In the New Testament, Paul reminds the believers in Rome that though we are saved by faith and not through living by the letter of the law, the law is not dead. 'Do we then overthrow the law by this faith? By no means! On the contrary, we uphold the law' (Rom 3:31 [RSV]).

It would be wrong to assume that unconfessed sin is always the cause of failure. It is only when we know what is right, but we decide to do the wrong thing and fail to confess our transgression, that God sometimes allows us to fail as a means of getting us back on the right track.

In my own case, after experiencing so much failure at something I had previously done successfully—my job—my only recourse was to cast myself before God and pray: I begged God to tell me why we had fallen on such hard times.

To be honest, I can't say I heard God's reply with my ears, but he clearly said, 'I allowed you to fail because you lied about your finances'. Stupidly, I began to argue with God, pointing out that it was only a matter of 200 dollars and that I hadn't even received the grant. I 'heard' the voice say again with gentle persistence, 'I was very disappointed by your lack of faith in me. Why do you say you trust me, then try to gain money on your own terms?' This wasn't the thundering voice of an enraged Jehovah who stood poised with his fist clenched ready to annihilate me—this was the gentle voice of the acknowledged authority of my life, the one whom I had invited into my heart, the one who says, 'My grace is sufficient for you' (II Cor 12:9 [RSV]). I was convicted and felt ashamed of how I had abused my freedom in Christ. Had I been an Old Testament character, I might have been reduced to a smouldering heap of ash for my bold-faced lie. Instead, financial failure reminded me of my dependence on God. Because God loves me, he had to treat me as a wise and loving parent would treat a disobedient child.

I went directly to my wife who had suffered along with me for the many weeks I had harboured my unconfessed sin. I told her what I had done and what I felt God had said. We embraced, and then I fell on my knees and offered my confession up to God. I didn't hear any reply this time, but I knew the matter had been taken care of. The words of Hebrews came home clearly to me as I knelt:

> And have you quite forgotten the encouraging words God spoke to you, his child? He said, 'My son, don't be angry when the Lord punishes you. Don't be discouraged when he has to show you where you are wrong. For when he punishes you, it proves that he loves you. When he whips you, it proves you are really his child.' Let God train you, for he is doing what any loving father does for his children. Whoever heard of a son who was never corrected? (Heb 12:5–7)

Since we were both on our knees, my wife suggested we asked God if he would provide a place for us to live as we would be out on the street imminently. Judith described to God our needs and what she hoped for, just as Catherine Marshall recommends we ought to in her book, *A Man Called Peter*.[1]

Although ours was a modest request, I honestly didn't expect God to act so quickly. Within a fortnight, we were living in two rooms which met almost exactly Judith's specific requests. I've added this story to give a balance: God will send failure into our lives to correct us, but—like any loving parent—God is also faithful and good. He answered our prayers at a time when we particularly needed renewed strength and a reinforcing of our faith. The story does not have a fairy-tale ending. Since earning my Masters Degree in 1984, I have spent long months unemployed in between freelance jobs. Just this week I had lunch with a friend who said, 'I really envy you. You're your own boss—you aren't locked into a rut like I am. How I wish I didn't have to punch a time clock!'

'The grass is always greener,' was my only reply, fighting back the urge to tell him my wife and I had just been arguing about the fact that neither of us have life insurance, a pension scheme, a savings account, nor the promise of steady work from month to month. Although I appear to be 'my own boss' because I do freelance work, in fact I'm one of the millions of people in Britain who cannot—and at this rate, so it seems, will not—find a steady full-time job. Yet, I trust I am still where God wants me and doing his will as best I am able.

This story may not be satisfactory to some Christians who are in the midst of a black and seemingly endless crisis, far more serious than any I've ever faced. Sometimes, endless self-examination and confession of sin seems to be of no help. I must stress that unconfessed sin is not the cause of all failure. The preservation of our humility and the outworking of God's ultimate plan for our lives—these, too, are reasons why Christians may fail. I will discuss further causes in later chapters. However, my point in this chapter still stands: when Christians know they have sinned, it is important that they do not try to rationalise their sins away—or worse, try to justify them as I tried to do. No one can predict what God will or will not do in different cases, but in my own case I knew that applying for that grant was the wrong thing to do, and God wanted me to own up to it.

To balance this point, there are many times when we sin and are not punished because Jesus has already taken our punishment when he died on the Cross.

## Actions Speak Louder Than Words

God often allows failure in order to discipline Christians who knowingly abuse their Christian liberty. A curate friend of mine once pointed out to me that Christians are often the only Bible some people will read. That means even our smallest actions—public or private—may affect an unbeliever's perception of the God we say we serve. Sinclair Lewis' novel, *Elmer Gantry*, and the film *The Mission* are good examples of how hypocritical Christians may actually drive people away from the saving light of the gospel. Therefore, God sometimes will chide and correct us—whether through failure or by other means—when we decide to sin. Volitional and unconfessed sin is anathema and has always called for speedy and radical surgery if there is to be a continued relationship between us and God. Thus Paul writes to the church in Rome, 'You are so proud of knowing God's laws, *but you dishonour him by breaking them.* No wonder the Scriptures say that the world speaks evil of God because of you' (Rom 2:23–24).

## The Prosperity Gospel?

With regard to our behaviour, we are now free to keep the law merely as a means of honouring our righteous God, not to earn our way into heaven. Ironically, as a result of the unheard of liberties we enjoy as Christians, there is a growing belief that God intends only the very best for his children—the best educations, the best homes, the best cars, the best jobs—the list can be endless. The principle is put forward that for a Christian to achieve anything less than the very best can only mean one thing: a loss of favour with the Father. In the light of the New Testament meaning of grace—unearned merit or favour—many Christians have been taken in by a false promise of prosperity. Most distressing is our anger towards God when we fail: we often believe that a thriving congregation in our church, a happy marriage, a meaningful relationship—success at whatever we do—is our right. Distress, disappointment and guilt can be the only fruits of this misguided philosophy.

Many Christians today live as if they are totally above experiencing failure by virtue of their faith. They pluck passages from the Bible (for example, Psalm 1) and then set out expecting to flourish, as if by magic. These people choose passages to back up this wishful thinking as well—for example, Proverbs 3:6: 'In everything you do, put God first, and he will direct you and crown your efforts with success.'

Christians are guilty of gross ignorance or outright manipulation if they blithely pick and choose their Scripture passages, selecting only the ones which promise health, wealth and success, but eschewing the darker passages which teach how we are accountable for our sins: 'There will be sorrow and suffering for Jews and Gentiles alike who keep on sinning' (Rom 2:9); '[Christians] must enter into the kingdom of God through many tribulations' (Acts 14:22), etc.

While Britain has yet to see the likes of the Revd Terry Cole-Whittaker, a self-styled evangelist of good tidings and material prosperity who reached public attention a few years ago in California, it will not be long before her brand of evangelism is heard in British pulpits. In 1984, *Newsweek* labelled the Revd Terry as the 'high priest of yuppidom'.

After attending one of her 'services' in California some years ago, writer Lloyd Billingsly quotes the Revd Terry as saying, 'Why shouldn't you be the wealthiest person on this planet and everybody just as wealthy as you? ... I teach money ... it's energy.' Billingsly's article continues, 'She derides a God that would allow germs to alight on people and thus cause disease; or a God that would allow such catastrophes as ruptured water heaters to disturb the serenity of his creatures.'[2]

The Revd Terry may be extreme, but she is not unique. Many Christian ministers make Jesus into a radical sociologist or political leader. This, too, is a form of prosperity gospel. Thankfully, dynamic ministers such as Luis Palau, Billy Graham, Mother Teresa and Michael Green do not propound the 'prosperity gospel'. However, those who *do* support the prosperity gospel are usually highly vocal, commanding media attention, with large, dedicated followings. In a world demanding irrefutable proof of God's goodness before moving to faith, prosperity theology stands apart from orthodox Christianity by demanding tangible evidence of God's goodness. Using logic based on human reason, the most comfortable parts of the Bible and gems from other religious writings, ersatz spiritual leaders think they are improving God's reputation by insisting that God promises to deliver the world from the pains of social injustice, want, despair and failure.[3]

Teachers who preach that a good God would never allow failure, pain and suffering to enter his creation have either ignored or forgotten that Jesus himself was pressed by evil men who expected to see a display of his power at his trial before they murdered him. Our Lord declined, saying no sign shall be given this generation—even though it made Christ himself appear to be a failure (Matt 12:39).

God does not do the bidding of men. We cannot manipulate nor decide God's will for his creation. In CS Lewis' *The Last Battle*, Aslan, a Christ symbol, appears to be uncaring about the hopeless plight of his Narnian followers. When the ancient holy trees are being cut down, apparently as a result of Aslan's orders, and the traditional enemy of the Narnians—the Calormenes—are made masters of the land, serious questions regarding Aslan's goodness are raised. Even the faithful ones are ready to assume the worst about the Mighty Lion. Jewel, the unicorn, asks Tirian, the King of Narnia, 'But, Sire, how *could* Aslan be commanding such dreadful things?'

'He is not a *tame* lion,' said Tirian. 'How should we know what he would do?'[4]

Perhaps Lewis had in mind the lesson of the suffering Job who, although innocent of any hidden sins, questioned God's goodness only to be humbled greatly when God put his own questions to Job. 'Do you still want to argue with the Almighty? Or will you yield? Do you—God's critic—have the answers?' (Job 40:2). Job was overwhelmed at the presence of the Lord and humbled at the majestic and mysterious workings of the universe. Job accepted that there were matters too difficult for him to understand:

> I know that you can do anything and that no one can stop you. You ask who it is who has so foolishly denied your providence. It is I. I was talking about things I knew nothing about and did not understand, things far too wonderful for me.... I loathe myself and repent in dust and ashes. (Job 42:2–3, 6)

The Christian God is not a tame God. He does not necessarily act according to our human expectations of him, however much it might seem fitting and right that he should. Joshua said to God after the sound defeat at Ai, 'For when the Canaanites and the other nearby nations hear about it, they will surround us and attack us and wipe us out. And then what will happen to the honour of your great name?' (Josh 7:9) This is the essence of mankind's unbelief: excessive concern with outward appearances. A truly sovereign God—that is, a God who is completely in control of the events of history—does not worry about public opinion polls.

When we see failures which cause pain and grief, our response is often to turn on God, demanding an explanation—or worse—that he vindicate his honour; once again Jesus replies, 'There shall be no sign given.' The testimony of the Scriptures is where we should seek our answer, for in the Scriptures we see that God does stand shoulder to shoulder with us in our pain by virtue of God's becoming a man, Jesus Christ. Through Christ, God is able to identify with every man, woman and child who has ever failed or will fail in this life. God is not unmoved by the pain and suffering which has become our legacy as the

result of Adam's fall. Sin is a terrible stigma and has—
to use a term used by Francis Schaeffer—'cracked the
image of God in man.' By this Schaeffer meant that
while we are still created in God's image, our nature is
altered, like the reflection in a cracked mirror, because of our sin. For those among us who are impatient
with the by-products of sin—war, crime, disease, failure—we may be certain that Christ, too, longed to
end all suffering with a snap of his fingers. But because
of the hardness of our hearts, it has to be done the
Father's way. Try to imagine Jesus' bitter frustration
when he lamented,

> O Jerusalem, Jerusalem, the city that kills the
> prophets, and stones all those God sends to her!
> How often I have wanted to gather your chil-
> dren together as a hen gathers her chicks be-
> neath her wings, but you wouldn't let me. And
> now your house is left to you, desolate. For I tell
> you this, you will never see me again until you
> are ready to welcome the one sent to you from
> God.                              (Matt 23:37–39)

We have been considering how God is able to use
our sin, our failings, and even our pain to bring about
his own plans for our individual good and the good of
humanity. To refute this is to reject the whole biblical
revelation of God. We cannot give God a character
different from that portrayed in the Bible; we cannot
make God as we think he should be, omitting those
parts we find difficult to swallow. Those who support
the prosperity gospel are doing just this, as indeed are
any who gladly accept the blessings, but reject the sufferings which are not spears and arrows sent from God
to harm us, but rather the outcome and result of the
fallenness of creation.

## The Christian Success Factor

Although it may be hard to comprehend, the 'successful' Christian life must include a fair amount of heartbreaking failure. How can a Christian be a failure and successful at the same time? The victorious Christian life is not the one *free* from pain and failure, rather it is the one that can accept and be transformed by failure —even the failure that leads to death. This may be called the 'Christian success factor.'

In the book *William's Story*, Rosemary Attlee describes the black despair which engulfed her family after her 17-year-old son, William, was given less than a month to live due to acute leukaemia. Rosemary chronicled the frustration and the feeling of being a failure as she stood by, unable to help, as her strong and handsome son was withering away and dying.

By her own admission, Rosemary wouldn't have called hers a Christian family, so it came as quite a surprise when William told his mother that he wanted to give his body and soul to God. A vicar cousin of the Attlee family came and counselled the boy. Rosemary stood transfixed outside the door, unable to hear the conversation, but from the sounds of laughter that issued from the sick-room, she judged the talk had been successful. Before leaving, the cousin prayed over William, rebuking the sickness in the name of Christ—a prayer neither William nor his mother had ever heard before. Soon after this, the local vicar came to the Attlee home and administered Communion once a week. According to Rosemary, this not only ministered to William, but it also helped the family come to terms with his terminal illness.

Some months later the medical consultant pronounced the cancer to be miraculously in remission, though he held firmly to the earlier diagnosis that William was dying. Over the next year, William read as much as he could about the Christian faith. He wrote a daily journal in which he detailed his anger and depression as well as the joy of his newly-discovered faith in a good God. Despite being emaciated and covered with purple spots where capillary blood vessels were leaking, William gradually found an uncanny peace which defies all human understanding through his decision to accept his illness as God's will for his life.

One cold November afternoon, the young man, a shadow of his former self, called both of his parents into his room to say his final goodbye. Rosemary took up his cold hand in her own as William murmured his last words. Seconds later he died.

> Before breaking the news to the rest of the family [we] sat alone together in the adjoining room. We had no sense of loss; that would come later. We felt shock—and gratitude. For in those agonising years our whole lives had been enriched by a knowledge to sustain us through the times ahead: we had learnt to accept whatever comes with hope, knowing Jesus is always able to bring good out of evil. The power of his Cross can bless all of our hardship and pain. Without him suffering can destroy, but with him it brings life, his life more abundantly.[5]

Joni Eareckson is paralysed from her neck down—the result of a swimming accident in the Chesapeake Bay when she was in her teens. In one painful moment her happy, active life turned upside-down and became filled with anguish. In some ways it might have been better had she been killed instantly. One of my own personal dreads is that one day I might become crippled or horribly maimed in some way. I doubt if I would find it easy to see God's goodness in such an untoward situation. Yet, soon after Joni realised she would spend the rest of her life bound to an iron wheelchair, God began a new work in her, giving Joni a desire to learn more about the spiritual side of life which she had previously ignored.

Although Joni admits to feeling trapped by her infirm body and in many ways feels cheated by what has happened to her, she has faced her failures head-on. Instead of dwelling on the tragic side of her accident, Joni fought to discover what she could and could not do in order to regain some modicum of normal living. Over the years, Joni has been flinging all of her energies into giving glory to God through her books, her mouth-held pen and ink sketches, and her spoken testimony—*despite* her handicaps.

For William, for Rosemary, for Joni, indeed for all of us who suffer crushing defeats, there is a choice we must make: we may choose bitterness and despair, or a life with new-found, unexpected and *different* joy. The Christian success factor is radically different from the world's success factor. Just contrast the prosperity gospel with Paul's words which proclaim,

> I know how to live on almost nothing or with everything. I have learned the secret of contentment in every situation, whether it be a full stomach or hunger, plenty or want; for I can do everything God asks me to with the help of Christ, who gives me the strength and power.
>
> (Phil 4:12–13)

These words indicate that walking with God does not promise a life of successful victories in the eyes of the world. Walking with God allows for the possibility of failing: we may fail, but with his help, we may 'fail successfully', to borrow a catchy phrase from the book by Jill Briscoe.[6]

None would dare call living with pain, hunger or poverty the hallmarks of achievement in a contemporary culture which grabs for all the outward trappings of success. In our society, living without things as basic as food and shelter are signs of failure. If Paul were alive today, I wonder how many of our churches would stand with him through the grim social failure of being a convict? I don't mean merely grabbing for our cheque-books to send the convict a gift of money —I mean how many of us would go down to the prison to lend him support physically, mentally and emotionally?

In 1977, I moved back to the United States and took a teaching job in Cecil County, Maryland. Although I am a Roman Catholic, I began attending a nearby Baptist church after having been invited there by a member of the congregation. One Sunday in August, a man asked if I'd care to join him and some others in visiting the local prison. Without hesitating, I said I would.

That afternoon I and nine other men met in the warden's office. From there we were led down a series of dimly lit corridors and stairways. It was hot and there was a rank odour in the air—a mixture of perspiration, disinfectant and stale tobacco. The further down into the prison we went, the stronger the odour grew, and the heat became almost oppressive. Outside it was a broiling 80°F. Inside this hell-hole it must have been close to 100°F. Large fans were set up to keep the fetid air circulating, but all they did was circulate the hot, humid atmosphere from one end of the cell block to the other.

Obviously, I had seen too many Hollywood films because I expected to find large cells holding men in crisp prison uniforms lounging on spartan, but neatly made-up camp-beds. When we reached our destination, I faced row upon row of 10-foot by 12-foot cells, each containing clusters of 6 adults in various stages of dress. The men lay on hard, tattered bunks stacked one above the other like book shelves. None of the inmates wore shirts, and many wore only grimy pants. The walls of the cells had once been painted drab grey, but most of the paint had been chipped or peeled away. The bare patches were covered with erotic drawings done in coloured felt-tipped pen. Elsewhere were telephone numbers for cheap sex, and slogans—lots of slogans: 'Jesus Saves', 'F—— the System', 'Eat S—— —a million flies can't be wrong'.

There was a black-and-white television set in each cell, and as we tried to read Scripture or talk to the men, their hard, passive eyes never strayed from the screens.

After an hour of what I considered sheer futility in terms of trying to reach these men with the salvation message of Christ, I was ready to return to the comparatively cool air and the green trees of the streets outside. Our leader, a stocky man with close-cropped grey hair, opened up a satchel he had been clutching in his hand. He handed out hymnals, suggesting we sing a few hymns before we left. Judging by the hateful glances of the sullen and uninterested men, I couldn't believe we were going to sing inspirational songs to them as well!

When the singing was over, the most unlikely looking man in one of the cells came forward and—pressing his face up to the bars and ignoring the curses of his five mates—he asked how he could receive Christ into his life. Even though I was thunder-struck by this conversion, I never set foot in that jail again. As I wrote in my journal on August 7th, 1977:

I know it was God's prompting and not mine or anybody else that made that man come forward (to commit his life to serving Christ). I don't know how this act of faith will affect that man's life, nor the lives of the others in his cell. How will he feel by the middle of this week? Will he still be a Christian? Or will the scorn of the other men get to him? Only God will know. I'd like to visit that guy during the weeks coming, but I know I won't. I don't have the courage to go into that prison again. I was never so glad to get back to my clean little world and my comfortable little ways.... I feel a horrible, horrible failure and a phony Christian. God forgive me.

Paul calls out to us over the misty, grey centuries and his voice speaks for countless prisoners around the world, particularly those in prison for their faith:

Please come as soon as you can, for Demas has left me. He loved the good things of this life and went to Thessalonica. Crescens has gone to Galatia, Titus to Dalmatia. Only Luke is with me.... The first time I was brought before the judge no one was here to help me. Everyone had run away. I hope that they will not be blamed for it.              (II Tim 4:9–11, 16)

Although we may not be fooled by the prosperity gospel, most of us would rather forget the suffering side of Christianity; ignoring the pain of the Christian couple whose unwed teenage daughter is pregnant; turning a blind eye to the wife whose husband has run off with the church organist; avoiding that man at our church who suffers from chronic depression—yes, forgetting that Christians do find themselves behind prison bars, too. Christians often prefer to align themselves with the winners in a society which denigrates failures. God abhors such an attitude.

In the introduction to his book *The Suffering and the Glory,* vicar David Prior writes:

> About 20 years ago I was asked to write an article for one of the national Church newspapers. It was intended, I think, to show how my call to ordination had evolved and to explain what made me tick. I remember framing my remarks around St Paul's great statement of personal ambition—'that I may know him and the power of his resurrection' (Phil 3:10 [RSV]). There is little I should want to change if I had to write a similar article today—but there is a lot I should have to add. Much of the additional material would, I trust, be a commentary on what Paul went on to say, but which I omitted: '… and may share his sufferings, becoming like him in his death'[7]

Prior adds that emphasising the glory minus the suffering has undermined the credibility of Western Christianity in a world which is suffering deeply—through famine, violence, oppression, unemployment and sickness. Prior argues for a balanced approach to living the Christian life. We hear so much about eating well-balanced diets these days: Christians would do well to accept that the well-balanced Christian life includes a fair amount of suffering—whatever the reason for that suffering.

If you are a Christian who has set out to serve God but has somehow failed and are suffering pain as a result, then the last thing you need to do is add to your suffering by believing God has abandoned you, or that he is bent on punishing you. Keep in mind that Satan wants to turn you against God. Paul points out, 'We are pressed on every side by troubles, but not crushed and broken. We are perplexed because we don't know why things happen as they do, but we don't give up and quit. We are hunted down, but God never abandons us' (II Cor 4:8–9).

Success and failure in our undertakings should never be the barometer to measure our walk with God. If you absorb one point alone from this chapter, let it be that the Christian God is not a vindictive God. There are reasons why pain and failure enter into our lives, but these reasons are God's reasons. We can never hope to fully explain or understand the twists and turns our life can take. So far, we have examined three reasons why Christians sometimes fail. Failure keeps us humble. And when we are humble, we are more likely to look to the Cross for our strength and purpose—as in the case of CS Lewis. What is viewed as failure in the eyes of men and women is really often seen in retrospect as the beginnings of an unexpected victory—as in the case of David Armstrong and the apparent failure of his mission of reconciliation in Ulster. Indeed, the very Crucifixion itself was the ultimate failure in the eyes of men and women, but a true victory in the eyes of God and the future of humanity. Finally, God uses failure as a means of chastising us as a loving father would his son, calling us to repent, so that we are able to then get on with serving him by being salt and light in a tasteless and darkened world: 'But if we confess our sins to him, he can be depended on to forgive us and to cleanse us from every wrong' (I John 1:9).

It is important to remember that God does not necessarily reward us for being 'good' by showering us with successes which may be measured by the world's standards. All things taken together—both the good and the bad—work together for the best in the lives of Christians, providing, of course, that our aim is to serve God above all else in this life. Paul underlines this in Romans 8:28.

Looking optimistically ahead in no way discounts any of the trauma, pain or discomfort we feel when we fail. However, perhaps our situation will be eased somewhat if, when we fail, we shut our ears to Satan who stands ready to accuse God of being uncaring, insensitive and a liar. Always remember that no matter how bleak our situation is, God is already at work using the circumstances to strengthen and bless us in the long run. If we believe this is so, then we might be able to sing with conviction:

> Through all the changing scenes of life,
> In trouble and in joy,
> The praises of my God shall still
> My heart and tongue employ.[8]

### Notes

[1]Catherine Marshall, *A Man Called Peter* (Fontana: London, 1964).

[2]Lloyd Billingsly, 'I Preach Money', *Eternity* (February 1986), pp 27–31.

[3]The prosperity gospel emasculates the concept of faith as summed up by the author of Hebrews, 'Now faith is the assurance of things hoped for, the conviction of things not seen' (Heb 11:1 [RSV]).

[4]CS Lewis, *The Last Battle* (The Bodley Head Ltd: London, 1956), p 31.

[5]Rosemary Attlee, 'A Mother's Story', *Reader's Digest* (April 1984), p 115.

[6]Jill Briscoe, *How to Fail Successfully* (Kingsway Publications Ltd: Eastbourne, 1983).

[7]David Prior, *The Suffering and the Glory* (Hodder & Stoughton Ltd: London, 1985), p 9.

[8]*Hymns Ancient & Modern Revised* (William Clowes & Sons, Ltd: London), p 233.

# Chapter 3

# Joy Through Failure

### Shattered Hopes

Hal and Marie Lindesberg, a Christian couple of Norwegian descent, own a small farm out in the Plains of Minnesota. If you've ever read any of the Laura Ingalls Wilder stories (*The Little House on the Prairie* and *The Little House in the Big Woods*), you will know of the brutal, Siberian-like blizzards that come sweeping into that part of the world, bringing winter as early as October and keeping it lingering well into May.

One year the Lindesbergs had made a profit from the feeder pigs and all the other work on the farm was up to date. It was an auspicious reward for years of hard work. They decided to reinvest the profits in building up the herd instead of using the money for other needs around the farm.

Not long after they had bought more pigs, Hal found that 24 of those pigs had died of a mysterious virus. They were out there in the yard lying on their backs, and the next morning 42 more were dead. The last of the herd died about two days after that—this was the beginning of some hard times for the Lindesbergs. Their entire herd and all the profits from the previous year were lost in a matter of days.

James Herriot, well known for his memoirs as a Yorkshire veterinarian, tells about Frank Metcalfe, a steel worker who longed to be a Dales dairy farmer. After years of saving and planning, Metcalfe made the transition from city to farm when he bought a piece of property with ruined buildings and a primitive house.

In less than two years Metcalfe and his wife had repaired the walls, improved the grasslands, and built up a strong stock of cattle—no small feat for a newcomer to farming. Herriot says that he and Frank used to talk of how the neophyte farmer intended to build up the farm, eventually expanding his operation. Herriot, who had seen farmers come and go, never doubted that Metcalfe would do as he said.

One day Herriot was called out to investigate an outbreak of brucellosis on the Metcalfe farm. The disease was confirmed, and a newly purchased cow was discovered to be the one that had introduced it to the herd.

Despite Herriot's and Metcalfe's efforts to isolate the infection, it spread to the entire herd. According to Herriot:

> The end of Frank's story was not far away. Autumn was reaching into winter and the frost was sparkling on the steps of Skeldale House when he called one night to see me. We went into the big room and I opened a couple of bottles of beer.
>
> 'I thought I'd come and tell you, Jim,' he said in a matter of fact tone. 'I'm having to pack up…. I have three cows which calved normally out of the whole herd. The rest are a mucky, discharging, sickly lot with no milk worth talking about. I've got no calves to sell or keep as replacements. I've got nowt.'[1]

Before the winter was over, Frank and his family were gone as if they had never been there at all.

So far, we have investigated three sets of circumstances in which people may fail. There is a fourth reason why we don't succeed: often failure is the result of facing difficulties that are insurmountable, given our natural limitations. In the case of the Lindesbergs, it was Hal's decision not to sell off his stock when he had the chance that led to his failure. If he had sold, they would have had money in the bank plus and they would have been spared the loss of newly purchased livestock. Frank Metcalfe put his best effort into starting a new life for his family away from the smoky steelworks of the city. He tried, but failed, through no fault of his own. He simply ran out of money and had to return to the city.

We must resist the temptation to read too much into our failures; there are times when our failures are simply the result of human error. Those who succeed have often taken a gamble. The Lindesbergs and the Metcalfes are examples of gambles that did not pay off—both families *could* have become very successful, but factors beyond their control prevented success.

The failures of the Lindesbergs and the Metcalfes were not God's way of keeping them humble—they were not necessarily set-backs which would ultimately lead to some great spiritual victory; nor were they apparently the result of unconfessed sin. Rather, these failures were the result of human error and the effects of a powerful disease. Such events in no way deny God's control, but they give us other factors in the understanding of failure.

## More of Life's 'Shattered Dreams'

Writer Jack Clemo has known much failure since he became blind and deaf, the result of an unfortunate illness. Despite his handicaps, he continues to write. By the time Clemo was in his mid-thirties, he and his mother were living in abject poverty, his writing netting only a few pounds a year. In those days, his greatest frustration was not that writing was so difficult—with great effort, by pecking out one key at a time on an old typewriter given to him by a sympathetic friend, he still produced letters, poems and novels—it was the endless flow of rejection slips which hurt the most.

> 'I struggled for over 14 years to get my first novel published,' Clemo said earnestly. 'Finally, Chatto and Windus bought it. It did well, but since then they have rejected three of my other manuscripts—*Broad Autumn, Cactus On Carmel,* and *The Clay Verge....* I suppose *Wilding Graft* was all the religious fiction they wanted from me!'[2]

Of course, after Clemo became deaf his novel-writing career ended. But when Clemo's natural ear failed him, another ear began to respond to the rhythm and pitch of a different dimension: poetry. Though he no longer experiences the physical joys of sight and sound, God has used these failings to allow Clemo a clearer vision of faith. He writes:

> And so I am awake,
> No more a man who sees
> Colour in flowers or hears from birds a song,
> Or dares to worship where the throng
> Seek beauty and its old idolatries
> No altar soils my vision with a lax
> Adult appeal to sense
> Or festering harmonies' magniloquence.
> My faith and symbol shall be stark.[3]

Clemo converted to Christianity in his thirties, and since this conversion was so important to him, he frequently writes about matters of faith. By his own admission, he does not feel God has singled him out for hardship. Therefore, Clemo writes despite the inevitability of more failure.

Clemo's is a physical failure. There are Christians who suffer failure for political reasons. Christians in the West enjoy a cornucopia of civil and religious liberties. However, millions of Christians in Communist lands fail to enjoy even things we take for granted—freedom of speech, freedom to travel, enough to eat (let alone the extra perks over and above what is needed for a decent life).

In the Soviet Union, for instance, membership of any unofficial Christian organisation brings with it automatic reprisals from the Communist party.[4] Many unemployed doctors, academics and labourers are the victims of religious persecution. For Soviet people, choosing to be a Christian under a Marxist regime is tantamount to choosing social failure. Reading Alexander Solzhenitsyn helps us to appreciate this fact. His career as a writer began to grow during the more liberal post-Stalin years. This *glasnost* (openness) gave Solzhenitsyn ample opportunity to share his Christian and political insights with a wide Soviet audience. His books landed him in trouble with the authorities and led to censorship: the bitterest failure for any writer to face. Soon, news of his unfair persecution began attracting much negative opinion from the West. Wide exposure in the Western press ultimately led to his expulsion from the Soviet Union: the Soviets knew he would draw far less attention on the outside than the inside, so since 1976 he has been living in seclusion in Vermont, USA, where he currently is at work on a book about the 1917 Bolshevik Revolution.

Yet even today Solzhenitsyn faces another sort of failure. Scammell's biography, *Solzhenitsyn*,[5] makes it clear that while the exiled Russian writer is glad to be free of the repression he once knew, and he is pleased that he is reaching a wide readership in the West, he is deeply grieved by the treatment he has received from the government of his homeland. The books he wrote were meant to help undo some of the injustices that abound in the Soviet Union. In Russia, the famous expatriate is published by the limited underground press only. The majority of Soviets do not know what has happened to him and so do not read his work. Solzhenitsyn has, therefore, failed to achieve his main objective: writing books for his countrymen to read.

When Solzhenitsyn first arrived in the United States, he was hailed by the press and was held in high esteem by Republicans and Democrats alike. Solzhenitsyn's popularity waned following his forthright criticism of the shoddy moral climate he found there: it prompted him to warn Americans that their spiritual lassitude could lead that nation to a sound defeat at the hands of the Communists. The liberal press and the détente-at-all-costs Carter Administration found his gloomy forecasts unpalatable. Thus today Solzhenitsyn may be seen as a prophet welcome neither in his homeland, nor in his adopted one.

Irina Ratushinskaya is a poet whose career failed because she calls Jesus her Saviour. She was serving the maximum seven-year sentence for 'anti-Soviet agitation and propaganda' when she was taken from the hard-labour camp in Mordovia to Kiev for a period of 're-education'. Then suddenly she and her husband, Igor (a scientist) were allowed to come to Britain. According to the *Church Times*,

> It is thought that the extensive publicity her case [received] in the West played a part in the matter ... she remains as firm as ever in her stand that she was tried unjustly, and has no intention of pleading for clemency, despite the extremely precarious state of her health.

The report concludes,

> The Revd Dick Rodgers, the Birmingham
> priest who led the 'Irina Vigil' said that her
> heart condition [had] deteriorated: in her last
> weeks in the [prison] camp she had experienced
> searing chest pains inducing loss of conscious-
> ness. She refused to see a doctor for fear of
> being administered drugs, said Dr Rodgers.[6]

In London Irina released a statement in which she
said that

> to release prisoners here and there would not be
> enough: we want human rights all across the
> board.
>      The authorities have to allow more intellectual
> freedom at the moment, as they need more man-
> power for advances in science and technology.

However, she took the view that generally,

> the government will not out of its own kindness
> or free will bring about any democratisation of
> society. It can only be the result of pressure
> from outside.[7]

Speaking at Wheaton College (Illinois, USA), Billy
Graham commented on the suffering of Soviet Christians as he talked about his experiences behind the
Iron Curtain. 'I have learned so much from those
people,' Graham said. 'They pay a price, and the
depth of their commitment is beyond anything I have
seen in my travels. Some of God's greatest saints are
in that place.'[8]

What are we to conclude about Christians and others
who suffer because of various unavoidable, natural
and political failings? One is tempted to castigate God

for leading his people into such horrid circumstances. God would indeed be a villain and not a just God if he did lead his children into the belly of the Beast, as it were, only to abandon them to cruel and overwhelming circumstances. But God does help those who call on him to deal with the reality of facing insurmountable difficulties. It is quite wrong to suppose that Christians are left to struggle on when tough situations seem to defeat them, despite their prayers and their best efforts.

Irina Ratushinskaya and Alexander Solzhenitsyn have failed in the eyes of Russian society. This has much to teach us about not placing importance on success in the eyes of the world: success in the eyes of God should be our goal. I Samuel 2:30 promises, 'I will honour only those who honour me.'

Sir Fred Catherwood, Member of the European Parliament, speaking at the conference on Christian faith and economics in Oxford, told the gathered delegates there about a brilliant young Russian woman who, upon completing her studies at university, was seeking a post as a teacher. She felt prompted to point out on her job applications that she was a Christian, although she knew this would certainly make her a less desirable employee in the eyes of most headmasters.

Not surprisingly, out of some 20 job applications, she was rejected without even as much as an interview. Then one day a letter came from a school where she had already been rejected. It was from the headmaster, asking her to come and see him in person.

It transpired that the head was a local Party Secretary. After a routine interview with the woman, he became very candid, admitting,

> Year in and year out I am plagued with letters which are filled with lies from applicants keen to

find work as teachers. When I saw on your
application that you admit to being a Christian,
I suspected that everything else you wrote was
probably true.

At this point he eased his wooden chair back from
his desk, stood, and paced over to the window. Turning he said, 'You are exactly the type of person I want
teaching our young people, however—' and here his
voice trailed off. After a pause, he continued, 'If I give
you this job, I want you to promise you will not try to
influence your pupils with any Christian ideas. Do you
promise?'

Keeping a level gaze, the woman sat pensively for a
few moments before replying, 'I promise.' Then she
added, 'But what if the children ask me questions
about Jesus?'

Now it was the headmaster who had to think quietly
before giving his answer. Finally, he said, 'The job is
yours. And if the children ask you about your faith in
God, then you may answer their questions. But you
must not try to persuade them to accept your beliefs.'

If you saw the film *Chariots of Fire*, or if you read
*The Flying Scotsman* by Sally Magnusson,[9] you will recall the awkward situation Eric Liddell found himself
in when, during the 1924 Paris Olympic Games, he
learnt he was scheduled to run on a Sunday—something his staunch Calvinist upbringing would not allow
him to do. When he refused to run, he was taken to
task by the press and considered to be a traitor to his
British team-mates. Yet, because Liddell was determined to honour God, God did in fact honour him. It
was arranged by the Olympic committee that the 'Flying Scotsman', as he was dubbed, could run in a different event on a weekday instead. Although it was not
his usual event, he went on to win.

Should any think Liddell lived a charmed existence as a result of his bravely honouring God, it must be pointed out that he died a depressing death as a Japanese prisoner of war, miles away from his family. Yet there are those living today who recall Liddell's joyful giving of himself in the prison camp through his organising of sport, social activities and Bible studies for the many bored teenaged children who were held captive with him during World War II.

From what resources do people such as Solzhenitsyn, Irina Ratushinskaya, her husband Igor, the Christian school teacher and Liddell draw? How do they withstand the pain of failure and not cave in under severe pressure?

## The Comforter

*If you love me, obey me; and I will ask the Father and he will give you another Comforter, and he will never leave you.*                    (John 14:15–16)

Some of the most ironic events during World War II may be directly attributed to the workings of the Holy Spirit. Testimonies of military chaplains that tell of men's conversions and growth into spiritual maturity while facing repression, torture and even pain of death are too numerous to mention here. One of the best books I have read on the subject is Ernest Gordon's *Miracle on the River Kwai*.[10] Gordon's message is that where there is anguish in this world, there is God. One might say that suffering is the business of the *Paraclete*, the Comforter, the one who is 'called alongside'.

Catherine Marshall, in her book *The Helper*, writes of the terror she experienced when her husband, Peter, was struck down in mid-career with heart failure.

After the ambulance sped him away, she was left at home, helpless, with nothing to do but worry. Out of sheer frustration, she dropped on to her knees and prayed. She describes the event in detail:

> But my knees no sooner touched the floor than I experienced God as a comforting mother— something altogether new to me. There was the feeling of the everlasting arms around me and at the same time, waves of tenderness like warm holy oil being poured over me. It was the infinite gentleness of the loving heart of God, more all-pervading than any human mother's love could ever be. Later was to come the more masculine side of God's caring when he knew that I would need more than tenderness. Then he would give me the first instalment of the other side of his comfort —not only loving consolation, but strength.[11]

Those who have read *A Man Called Peter*[12] will know that although thousands of people around the world had been praying for the Revd Peter Marshall's recovery, he still died, leaving Catherine with a young son and no means of supporting herself. Catherine Marshall might have rightly asked God, 'Why me?' just as Job did when his suffering and losses became too much to bear. God never spoke to Catherine Marshall from a whirlwind as he did to Job, yet it is clear that the Lord's promise in Hebrews gave her the wisdom and courage to believe: 'I will never, *never* fail you nor forsake you' (Heb 13:5). Catherine's prayer gives us the key to a fuller understanding of how we may find victory through our painful failures:

> Father, I thank you that you have so lovingly provided a way to meet my every need, that you

and you alone satisfy all the deep and hidden hungers of my heart. You know how much I hurt. You see my unshed tears. I even battle bitterness sometimes, Lord. Take that away and give me comfort instead.

How I praise you for your gentleness to me. But even more, that you send me the [Comforter] to supply the strength I do not have, to undertake for me. Thank You Lord. Thank You. Amen.[13]

I have looked to the lives of others to identify how people cope with failure. On a personal level, I would be dishonest if I did not point out that I do not suffer failure gladly—nor even quietly. It could be symptomatic of my relatively young age. I know from my many older friends that when they experience failure, they don't panic. They just get on with life as best they are able. How? Because they have known other tragedies—some which left them numb with grief, others which turned out to be blessings in disguise—and they have learned how to trust God in all circumstances. This is truly the testimony of age and experience.

I'm thinking of people whom I've met over the years—for example, Mrs Rothman, who endured an abusive husband for 35 years, never thinking of divorcing him for the sake of her children, looking after her husband's needs until he committed suicide. Another example of people who endured terrible pain is the Lauden family, whose daughter's spinal meningitis was casually misdiagnosed as a cold, leading rapidly to her death as the parents looked on helplessly.

These friends are by no means immune to worry, but they long ago surrendered control of their lives to Christ. Along with control of their lives, they handed over control of their money, their health and their circumstances. All they possessed was exchanged for faith in a good God. This fact, combined with years of trusting him for all things—spiritual as well as physical—has brought them to an understanding that even failure can be part of a greater good in their lives. Paul teaches Christians to 'Put on all of God's armour so that [they] ... will be able to stand safe against all strategies and tricks of Satan.... In every battle you will need faith as your shield to stop the fiery arrows aimed at you by Satan' (Eph 6:11, 16).

Some people have great difficulty when it comes to placing faith in God: it seems to them difficult to place faith in the unseen. Yet don't we exercise faith each time we send of a cheque in the post, try out a new medicine prescribed by a doctor, or board a train or jet for a journey? I know in my own case, I don't conduct a full-scale investigation to be certain beyond a shadow of a doubt that everything will work according to my expectations. I just have faith that it will; so do most folk. That's how a society functions. And if we are able to have such great faith in man-made systems which we *know* are likely to fail sooner or later, shouldn't we be willing to have faith in a God whose promise is that he will never fail us (Heb 13:5)?

We have the Lord's promise that as soon as the worst moment of our life occurs, the Holy Spirit is already at work in our situation bringing us a peace which often passes our understanding:

> Don't worry about anything; instead, pray about everything; tell God your needs and don't forget to thank him for his answers. If you do this, you will experience God's peace, which is far more wonderful than the human mind can understand. His peace will keep your thoughts

and your hearts quiet and at rest as you trust in
Christ Jesus.                                    (Phil 4:6–7)

## But Does God Do What He Promises?

Certainly, if he is all powerful, God can wave his hand
and cause all human failings to evaporate. In one
moment all suffering would come to an end for his
followers. But nowhere in the Bible are we given a
*promise* that we will not have problems in this life. We
may be certain that while God is grieved by our failure
and pain, he will not override his own decree that man
shall be free indeed to love or reject him—in spite of
any untoward outward appearances. What if each
time we were in a tight spot, we could call on God to
save us? God would be nothing more than a slave, and
if history may be used as a guide, few men, if any,
loved their slaves and vice versa.

A brief look at the lives of the saints in the Bible will
reveal the unvarnished truth: when a man or a woman
sets out to love and serve God, suffering, failure and
pain are sure to be a part of the total experience of that
person's life. God's promise is that we will never have
to face any bad circumstances on our own.

## What's The Point In Allowing Anyone To Suffer?

Stephen was selected by the disciples soon after the
Resurrection to look after the needs of the widows of
the church. We are told by Luke that Stephen stood
out from the others in faith, grace, spiritual power and
wisdom (Acts 6:5, 8, 10). He was able to do miracles
and preach the gospel. He appeared to be a man
favoured of God—a man destined for great things.

Soon, however, Stephen ran foul of the local
synagogue, and the Sanhedrin charged him with blas-
phemy. At his trial he claimed to see Jesus standing at

the right hand of God: for this he was seized and duly stoned to death. What a terrible waste of a life! Yet, Saul of Tarsus, the future St Paul, assisted in Stephen's execution, and it was then that he first witnessed the remarkable 'peace that passes all understanding.' Instead of begging for mercy or shouting out in pain, '[Stephen] fell to his knees, shouting, "Lord, don't charge them with this sin!" and with that, he died' (Acts 7:60). Not long after, Paul's eyes were opened and he became a follower of Christ.

When Dietrich Bonhoeffer, the anti-Hitler Lutheran pastor, was executed in 1945, the Nazi doctor present said later that he had never seen a man die so peacefully, so entirely submissive to the will of God.[14]

The way Christians distinguish themselves under adverse conditions may open the eyes of the unbelieving. If this is so, then perhaps we can better understand why God allows for the suffering of his children. The power of the Christian God is evidenced through the response to suffering and failures by his Church. Writing an early history of the Church, Eusebius of Caesarea says of the Christians of the Second Century:

> … they are put to death, and they gain new life. They are poor, and make many rich; they lack everything, and in everything they abound. They are dishonoured, and their dishonour becomes their glory; they are reviled and they are justified. They are abused and they bless; they are insulted, and they repay insult with honour. They do good, and they are punished as evildoers; and in their punishment they rejoice as gaining new life therein
>
> (Eusebius, The Epistle to Diognetus V.13–17)

This does not play down the suffering felt by people

whose hopes appear to be shattered, but rather gives a sense of perspective in our moments of despair.

We must see that, far from the popular misconception perpetrated by ignorant or wilfully dishonest teachers, Christians are not entitled to justice and equality, nor to live lives of comfort and ease, free from set-backs and totally unacquainted with failures. While this does not mean Christians ought to expect suffering or go out of their way to find it, it does help give us a clearer understanding of our true position in the universe: in addition to the failings of human nature, we are up against 'principalities, against the powers, against the world rulers of this present darkness, against the spiritual hosts of wickedness in the heavenly places' (Eph 6:12 [RSV]).

In his book *Destined For The Cross*, Dr Paul E Billheimer argues that the essence of the Christian life is to identify with what is mistakenly viewed by the world as *the* single most colossal failure of the ages: the suffering, Crucifixion and death of Jesus Christ.[15]

*Jesus Christ, Superstar*, Andrew Lloyd Webber's and Tim Rice's popular musical which ran for years in the West End, proclaimed that Christ was at best a misunderstood tragic hero. That the play ends with the dramatic and poignant Crucifixion on Good Friday, and not with the victorious Resurrection of the following Easter Sunday speaks volumes about the gross misconceptions obscuring the message of Christianity. It is the humiliation of the Cross *plus* the joy of the Resurrection which bring victory to the Christian life.

### A Life Of Sackcloth And Ashes?

Having discussed the more sombre aspects of suffering, I would like to turn to what is often a powerful and dynamic consequence of failure: joy. In 1986, a widely publicised survey taken in Britain[16] found that most people consider the Church to be boring, outmoded and gloomy—an irony, since the victory on the Cross can mean only one thing for people: joy! In no other religion and in no other literature is joy so conspicuous as in Christianity and in the Bible.

Psalm 89:15 says, 'Blessed are those who hear the joyful blast of the trumpet, for they shall walk in the light of your presence'; then there is Luke 10:17: 'When the 70 disciples returned, they joyfully reported to him, "Even the demons obey us when we use your name";' and John 15:11: 'I have told you this so that you may be filled with joy'; and yet another example—I Thess 1:6: 'So you became our followers and the Lord's; for you received our message with joy from the Holy Spirit in spite of the trials and sorrows it brought you.' The references to joy go on and on. Take any concordance and look the verses up for yourself—you will find scores of them.

Several years ago, while my wife and I were students at English L'Abri, we were being counselled by Richard Winter. It was a tense session and all three of us felt the strain. All of a sudden there was a tapping at the door and in ran Richard's three-year-old daughter. Instead of fobbing her off with a hurried platitude, he opened wide his arms, and called her to him. Then he introduced her to Judith and me. Once he had done this, he asked her what she wanted. Of course all she wanted was her daddy. After planting a big kiss on her cheek, he explained how busy he was, but promised to come out to the kitchen to see her just as soon as he could. With this, he set her back on the floor and she tore out of the room, beaming ... and so were we!

This brings to mind the time Jesus was ministering

to the pressing needs of a crowd and some children were presented to him. When the disciples saw the children,

> [they] shooed them away, telling them not to bother him.
> But when Jesus saw what was happening, he was very much displeased with his disciples and said to them, 'Let the children come to me, for the kingdom of God belongs to such as they. Don't send them away! I tell you as seriously as I know how that anyone who refuses to come to God as a little child will never be allowed into his kingdom.'                (Mark 10:13–15)

In the book *The Humour of Christ*, theologian Elton Trueblood develops a good case for smashing the stuffy image of our Lord created by past generations of bad stained glass and even worse literature. Trueblood points out that if Jesus was actually a sombre and morose man, common people would have been repelled by him and children would have called him names. Since this was not the case, it stands to reason that Christ was probably a witty and pleasant man to be around. Granted, Christ was a man well acquainted with grief and sorrow, and he was one who knew about failure, yet he was still able to radiate the joy of life that drew all sorts of people to him—rich and poor, educated and uneducated, tall and small. How much more should Christians allow his joy to percolate in their lives, regardless of their circumstances? Despite their many trials and failures, sackcloth and ashes are not appropriate apparel for Christians. As the poets tell us, true joy is reserved for those who have suffered; true laughter comes only from one who has wept bitter tears.

## The Paradox Perceived

Here is a Christian paradox: ultimate victory is had by accepting defeat. Does this have a vaguely existentialist ring about it? Yes, were it not a Christian doctrine! Part of the existentialist theory is that the only value in life comes from being faced with the opposition—or absurdity—between man and what is not man.

The existentialist paradox is one that offers no hope: man finds meaning in his sorrows, but there is no promise of a life without suffering to come. This paradox may be summed up by the punch line at the end of Woody Allen's film *Annie Hall*—a line that might make us smile but which offers no hope for living—nor for dying or beyond:

> A—My wife thinks she's a chicken.
> B—So why don't you take her to a psychiatrist?
> A—[philosophically] I need the eggs.

## Existentialism: A Gateway To Hope?

The Christian paradox, however, offers us a gateway to hope. From her book of the same title, Maria Boulding writes:

> Christ's long, dark journey is ours, and ours is his. He is in us and we are in him. In no part of the journey and in no place of failure are we ever alone. It is joyful because of him; there is great beauty along our road, and the certainty of his love.... Distress and bewilderment, knowing yet not knowing, the burning hearts, the realisation afterwards that amid all the unknowing, we did know the closeness of Christ in Word and sacrament: all this is an inspired

picture of how things are, since Easter, along our road. He is more than a wayfarer with us; he is the Way.[18]

In Albert Camus' *La Peste*,[19] Père Paneloux pronounces that the bubonic plague originates as a punitive act of God. Thus, as Camus sees it, if we attempt to resist evil, we are forced to choose between fighting God (who created the plague) or join God in persecuting man by passively accepting evil. Commenting on Camus' existential polemic, Francis Schaeffer writes,

> It simply is not true that [man has] ... to side with the doctor against God by fighting the plague, or join with the priest on God's side and thus be much less than human by not fighting the plague. If this were an *either/or* choice in life, it would be truly terrible. But the Christian is not consigned to such a choice. Let us go to the tomb of Lazarus. As Jesus stood there, he not only wept, but he was *angry*. The exegesis of the Greek of the passages John 11:33 and 38 is clear. Jesus, standing in front of the tomb of Lazarus, was *angry* at death and at the abnormality of the world; the destruction and distress caused by sin.[20]

The point is, we live in a fallen and sinful universe which opens us to the absurd consequences of sin: pain, hurt, failure (Rom 6:23). What Camus may not have realised is that Jesus hates the plague, as well. More importantly, to affirm his solidarity with his creation, God became man and endured his own death, that great equaliser and ultimate failure, to demonstrate once and for all his love for humanity. In doing so, he also threw open the formerly barred gateway to eternal life in fellowship with the Father in heaven.

In what remains for me one of the most telling scenes from Woody Allen's film *Hannah and Her Sisters*, Allen is seen unloading a sack of religious icons during his quest to find meaning for his unsatisfactory life. The last item in the sack—a loaf of highly refined, preservative-filled, white pre-sliced bread in a plastic bag—leaves the viewer with little doubt about Allen's pessimistic scepticism regarding Jesus' promises for the next life.

Conversely, there is hope in the words of John, who writes, 'For God loved the world so much that he gave his only Son so that anyone who believes in him shall not perish but have eternal life' (John 3:16).

Sadly, many of the artists and writers of this century do not grasp the significance of Christ's sacrificial love. Christ's life would indeed have been the tragedy of *Jesus Christ, Superstar*, had it not been for the miracle of the empty tomb which the Apostles' Creed treats as historical fact, despite what some learned theologians are saying to the contrary.

### Our Cross

In Matthew 10:28, 16:24, 27:32; in Mark 8:34; and in Luke 9:23, 14:27, Jesus unequivocally states the central importance of submitting to God's will. Like it or not, the Christian life calls for a share of suffering:[21]

> Then be happy, for when the way is rough, your patience has a chance to grow. So let it grow, and don't try to squirm out of your problems. For when your patience is finally in full bloom, then you will be ready for anything, strong in character, full and complete.     (James 1:2–4)

### Fear No Evil

With the help of the Comforter, and with the faith in the promise of our own resurrection day, and—not least importantly—the help of other Christians to rally and support us in our failure, there is a ray of hope for those in despair: there is an answer to their pain —the pain of depression, the pain of persecution, the pain of our failure. It is truly comforting to know that there is the possibility of rejoicing even in adversity.

### Together We Will Stand

Martin and Anne are a Christian couple who live in a small village. One day Martin walked out on Anne for a much younger woman, leaving three children for his wife to raise on her own. Martin never returned to their church, although Anne continued to bring the children. What's more, many of the women in the village reached out to comfort Anne: they invited her to shop with them, wept with her when she felt the need, and—this perhaps is the most significant of all—they treated her as if she were normal.

One day Anne asked her vicar if she could speak briefly to the congregation at the end of a service. Standing bravely before the others she quoted these words from the hymnal:

> Faint was I, and fears possessed me,
> Bruised was I from many a fall;
> Hope was gone, and shame distressed me:
> But His love has pardoned all.
> Days of darkness still may meet me,
> Sorrow's paths I oft may tread;
> But His presence still is with me,
> By His guiding hand I'm led.[22]

Although Anne was close to tears, they were the tears neither of fear nor self-pity, rather they were the tears of a profound gratitude both to God and to the people of the church. Satan would have loved Anne to blame herself for her failed marriage, making her feel bitter towards God. Amazingly, this was not the case.

Later on, many people waited at the door to hug and console Anne. It is so important for Christians to affirm and uphold each other. This is a recurring theme in Paul's letters to the various churches. God invites his people to work in tandem with him. All Christians are obliged to reach out and offer assistance when they see others failing in some way. There is a beautiful image in the Gospels to remind us to bear one another's crosses. Matthew and Luke tell us that one Simon of Cyrene (North Africa) was compelled to help Christ as he carried his cross-piece along the road to his Crucifixion.

To sum up then, failure brings humility, pain and suffering which give us the chance to demonstrate to the watchful world the power of the Cross as we endure all things for Christ's sake with the help of the Holy Spirit. Paradoxically, it is the power of the Cross which brings life to a dying world. Christians are not spared humiliating failures, nor are they to isolate themselves from the failures and grim circumstances of others. They are called to participate fully:

> When one thrusts himself deeply into life, and lives it to the fullest, there is bound to be failure. To enjoy life one must not shrink from it, but accept it as it is. 'For God hath not given us the spirit of fear; but of power, and of love.' And we can walk before the Lord in the land of the living.[23]

## Notes

[1]James Herriot, *All Things Bright and Beautiful* (Michael Joseph Ltd: London, 1976), p 308.

[2]Michael A Apichella, 'Interview With a Rebel', *The Christian Writer* (January 1985), p 24.

[3]*ibid* p 25.

[4]'Russian Christians Reproach the West', *Church Times* (August 29th, 1986), p 3.

[5]Michael Scammell, *Solzhenitsyn* (Hutchinson & Co, Ltd: London, 1985).

[6]'Irina Allowed to See Husband', *Church Times* (August 15th, 1986), p 1.

[7]'Irina to Stay in West for Time Being', *Church Times* (December 26th, 1986), p 16.

[8]Patricia Swindoll, 'Graham Offers Answers and Advice', *Inform—Bulletin of Wheaton College* (Winter 1986), p 1.

[9]Sally Magnusson, *The Flying Scotsman* (Quartet Books Ltd: London, 1981).

[10]Ernest Gordon, *Miracle on the River Kwai* (Tyndale House: Wheaton, IL, 1984).

[11]Catherine Marshall, *The Helper* (Chosen Books: Waco, Texas, 1978), p 113.

[12]Catherine Marshall, *A Man Called Peter* (Fontana: London, 1964).

[13]Catherine Marshall, *The Helper*, p 113.

[14]Norman Hare, 'Fresh Light on Bonhoeffer', *Church Times* (September 19th, 1986), p 9.

[15]Paul E Billheimer, *Destined For The Cross* (Tyndale House: Wheaton, IL, 1983).

[16]Marplan Survey commissioned by *Sunday Express*— reported in *Church Times* (December 12th, 1986), p 1.

[17]Elton Trueblood, *The Humour of Christ* (Darton, Longman & Todd Ltd: London, 1965).

[18]Maria Boulding, *Gateway to Hope* (Fount: London,

1985), p 140.

[19]Albert Camus, *The Plague* (Hamish Hamilton Ltd: London, 1948).

[20]Francis Schaeffer, *The God Who is There* (Hodder & Stoughton Ltd: London, 1968), p 107.

[21]In CS Lewis' *The Great Divorce*, two theologians meet in a transitional place between heaven and hell. Dick is one of the 'bright people' who is heaven bound, and the Ghost is a visitor from the city of death below. Dick points out that most of the doctrines which they had ignored in their early ministries, doctrines dealing with hell or the resurrection, were in fact true.

> 'Are you serious, Dick?'
>
> 'Perfectly.'
>
> 'This is worse than I expected. Do you really think people are penalised for their honest opinions? Even assuming, for the sake of argument, that those opinions were mistaken?'
>
> 'Do you really think there are no sins of intellect?'
>
> 'There are indeed, Dick. There is hide-bound prejudice, and intellectual dishonesty, and timidity, and stagnation. But honest opinions fearlessly followed—they are not sins.'
>
> 'I know we used to talk that way. I did it too until the end of my life when I became what you call narrow. It all turns on what are honest opinions.'
>
> 'Mine certainly were. They were not only honest, but heroic. I asserted them fearlessly. When the doctrine of the Resurrection ceased to commend itself to the critical faculties which God had given me, I openly rejected it. I preached my famous sermon. I defied the whole chapter. I took every risk.'
>
> 'What risk? What was at all likely to come of

it except what actually came—popularity, sales for your books, invitations, and finally a bishopric? ... Let us be frank. Our opinions were not honestly come by. We simply found ourselves in contact with a certain current of ideas and plunged into it because it seemed modern and successful. At College, you know, we just started automatically writing the kind of essays that got good marks and saying the kind of things that won applause. When, in our whole lives, did we honestly face, in solitude, the one question on which all turned: whether after all the Supernatural might not in fact occur? When did we put up one moment's real resistance to the loss of our faith?' ...

I'm far from denying [said the Ghost] that young men may make mistakes. They may well be influenced by current fashions of thought. But it's not a question of how the opinions are formed. The point is that they were my honest opinions, sincerely expressed.'

'Of course. Having allowed oneself to drift, unresisting, unpraying, accepting every half-conscious solicitation from our desires, we reached a point where we no longer believed the Faith.... But errors which are sincere ... are not innocent.'

(CS Lewis, *The Great Divorce* [Fontana: London, 1971]. Reproduced by kind permission)

[22]*Christian Praise* (The Tyndale Press: London, 1964), p 121.
[23]Jo James, *Don't Be Afraid* (Christian Literature Crusade: Fort Washington, PA, 1977), pp 12–13.

# Chapter 4

# Let Us Sow, That Others May Reap

**What Kind Of God?**

'And I am sure that God who began a good work within you will keep right on helping you grow in his grace until his task within you is finally finished on that day when Jesus Christ returns' (Phil 1:6).

My friend Nick tells a story of his parents' failed missionary career. They felt called to a church-planting project in a small village in Kenya. First, they secured permission from the local chief to settle near the main encampment. Soon after, they bought a small patch of land, built a hut, and without any of the modern tools of the West, they set about farming and trading with the villagers. Nick, being the first white baby these Africans had ever seen, was quite a novelty. His mother was never in need of a baby-sitter!

After five years, Nick's family had learned the language, and although they did not try to make converts, they had succeeded in piquing the curiosity of the old chief of the tribe. He wanted to know why a family of whites would want to settle amongst his tribe. Nick's father knew that the best possible answer would be the honest one: 'We came because our God directed my footsteps here.'

This reply made a great deal of sense to the chief, and at his request, Nick's father was invited to build a chapel and conduct services in the African dialect. This way, the people could hear and decide for themselves what kind of God Nick's father worshipped.

In the next five years, six tribesmen made commitments to Jesus, about whom Nick's father had preached. On the face of it, 6 converts in 10 years might not seem like a success story—but of the 6 converts, 1 was the son of the chief. Before long, more and more people began coming to the church services, until—finally—the chief himself came one Sunday, proclaiming, 'I have seen a change in too many of my people!' Nick's father held his breath, thinking perhaps the chief was offended by what had taken place in his village. The chief continued in his firm tone, 'And if worshipping your God can make *good* people better, then I, too, wish to know more of this Jesus from the East.' You can imagine the celebrations which took place in that tiny village that day!

Now, if the story had ended here, it would have the ring of success. But there is more. Shortly after this, Nick's parents were laid low by a serious illness. There were no medical facilities in that part of Kenya then as there are today, so a moratorium was called on all church activities as the two missionaries langished. Some of the tribesmen had taken this opportunity to point out that the old gods were expressing their indignation at the outsiders who were leading the tribe away from their traditional means of worship. Nick's father grieved deeply that he was too ill to disprove the gloomy pronouncements of the unbelievers. He had to stay helplessly in his sick-bed as one after another of the congregation went back to their former beliefs. Mustering all the faith they had, the missionaries began to pray that they would be healed so they could carry on the good work which they had begun.

Before too many months had passed, it became clear that if they remained in the village any longer, Nick's parents would surely die. Reluctantly, after 12 years of toiling, the disappointed missionaries abandoned their project, utterly dejected and angry at God.

Nick's story illustrates a point that we must never lose sight of as Christians: that just because we are carrying out God's will in the way he has called us, it does not exclude us from facing failure—especially failure caused by natural circumstances such as sickness and even death. In his book, *Circumstances and the Role of God*,[1] theologian John Boykin reminds us that it is wrong to expect God to intervene in our lives in an extraordinary manner. Of course it may be argued that the Bible records many extraordinary events, such as a talking mule, the parting of a sea, and lame people cavorting about when, moments before, they were flat on their backs. But Christians must take care not to expect miracles as a convenient means of escaping their sorrows or disappointments.

In my own life, I frequently find myself asking God to turn his hand to answering my unreasonable desires—perhaps to recharge a flat battery, or to miraculously transform a fail mark for an exam into a pass mark. In each case I am asking *God* to do *my* will. Each time I venture to do this, I am like the clay telling the potter what he may and may not do with his clay (see Romans 9:21).

We who are stuck in time and space, cannot see the course of world events from the Father's vantage point outside of the physical realm. It is quite natural to grieve over apparent failings. In fact, it is actually therapeutic to 'blow off steam' as it were, letting God know exactly how we are feeling about our situation, or asking him why certain things are happening in our lives. When we do this, however, we must endeavour not to give in to certain human temptations such as self-pity or pride. The temptations themselves are not sinful, but when we give in to them, sin comes between us and God.

In the Bible, Paul was given a 'thorn in [his] flesh'— a 'messenger from Satan'—to torment him. Being a normal man, he complained to God. It was no fun having this 'thorn', so he begged God to relieve his condition. However, when God clearly said, 'No', Paul acquiesced. Then, making the best of a bad situation, he turned his infirmity into an astute object lesson on spirituality to help fledgling Christians understand more about their God (II Cor 12:7–10). On this matter David Prior comments, 'Paul is ... creatively seeing suffering as an opportunity to prove the faithfulness of God.'[2] Clearly, Paul could have indulged in self-pity and that could have brought his ministry to a halt.

Let's return to my friend Nick. I don't blame his missionary father for being so upset: he poured 12 years of his life into a project which, on the brink of success, seemed to have fallen flat on its face. Then, summoning all his faith, he prayed to be made well enough to go on preaching the Word of God, but to no avail. What's more, he had tangible proof that the tribe was reverting back to animism, despite having made earlier professions to Christ. Anyone who can endure *that* without turning to God and shaking his fists in rage, is certainly a strong person.

As it happens, Nick was away at university when his father finally died. Nick's mother had told him in a letter that although his father continued to worship in church, he went to his grave an embittered and angry old man, blaming God for his crushing failure as a church-planting missionary. When God sanctions painful failure, Prior goes on to say, 'It is very possible to see it as ... a demonstration of the unfaithfulness and unfairness of God, with the result that we become bitter and depressed.'[3] However, this is seeing failure from a purely human point of view.

## From Africa With Love

Years later, Nick was back in East Africa working for a multinational company. Quite by chance, he and his colleagues found themselves within 50 miles of the village where Nick had spent much of his childhood. Hiring a Land Rover, he and a few friends made their way across the bush to pay a visit to the village.

Nick guessed the place would be changed. In his childhood the village had been relatively untouched by Western influences, but now the children would probably be wearing jogging outfits and listening to Walkman radios. There would be modern technology and some modicum of prosperity. The last thing Nick expected to see was any evidence of his father's church work.

Upon arriving, it was as he had thought: there was now an oiled road, wells, and the bush had been cleared to make way for corn and wheat crops. There were the expected Western additions, including a few brick buildings—but to Nick's utter amazement, one of the brick buildings was a church.

Before long, Nick was reacquainted with some of his childhood friends who had remembered him. Over a meal, Nick told of how his father had eventually died, but that he and his mother still thought about the village.

The pastor of the church had come especially to meet Nick. When the meal was over, the clergyman stood up to speak: 'I came specifically to meet the son of the man who brought the Good News to a dying village!' Nick sat in stunned silence as he listened. 'After your family left us,' the pastor said as he stood, 'quite naturally the church fell on hard times. But before the work was completely lost, one of the first men your father baptised took over as pastor. It was sad that your family had gone back to England, but under this man's leadership, the church was saved and even prospered.'

In addition, Nick learned that the church had had an unbroken series of pastors who came from within the village or nearby. This, they maintained, was God's way of showing everyone what kind of God they served: Jesus was Lord of all, even Kenya.

The pastor grinned broadly, exposing perfectly straight white teeth, saying, 'Now you go back and tell your mother this good news. Tell her it comes from Africa with love!'

The church Nick's father had expected to disintegrate was by that time sending out its own missionaries to other villages—grief and sorrow from the past had been turned to rejoicing.

This story serves as a reminder to us not to conclude in adversity that God has allowed us to fail for no reason at all. Tragically, Nick's father was too overcome with sorrow and bitterness to see that his role was like that of John the Baptist's—one called to baptise with water, or sow the seed—then to stand aside, allowing others to reap the harvest. In Chapter 6, I will discuss the similar experience of Moses—similar in that he was called to lead the Israelites out of bondage towards the Promised Land, but was never allowed to fulfil the task. Moses and Nick's father can both be seen as the sowers of seed. Nick trusts that his father can now see the fruits of his loyalty to and labour for God.

## The Cost Of Being A Christian

When God starts a good work, he sees it through to its conclusion, even if we must taste failure as part of the means to his ends. There is no shame or lasting sting if we see that failure, impotence and sorrow bring us back to the paradox of the Christian experience: 'My power shows up best in weak people ... when I am weak, then I am strong' (II Cor 12:9–10). If this is hard advice for us to follow, then that means we are beginning to appreciate the high cost of telling Christ that he may enter our lives and take charge.

We cannot believe for long that there is no price to pay when we follow the Lord—if we turn to the Bible. Think of Noah withstanding the jeers of his neighbours as he spent money to build a seafaring boat far inland when he could have been earning money trading. Consider Moses' humiliation when he was promised by God that he was to deliver his people from bondage. Yet under Moses the Jews wandered in a desert wasteland for 40 years before reaching the frontier of the Promised Land, hardly more than a fortnight's hard journey out of Egypt. In each case God's will was done, but both Noah and Moses had to overcome the derision of the people as they carried through the will of God.

## Bible Characters Are Too Remote

As already mentioned, when I sometimes cannot understand the circumstances of ancient biblical characters, I seek out older men and women in my church and talk to them about God's faithfulness in times of failure and adversity.

One woman, Mary, told me that years ago she and her husband had committed themselves to serving God. They agreed that they wanted to have a practical ministry, not just one of worship and prayer. One morning—not long after making this commitment—Mary's husband left for work but never came home. In a letter to her, he said he didn't love her any more and he wanted a divorce. While Mary never remarried, it was at this point that the adventure of living by faith began in her life.

Again and again, Mary had to trust God to provide the things her husband had always provided through his work. At first, she had to depend on the charity of friends. Soon, though, she became more independent of others—yet, says Mary,

> There were times when I was sure I was about to go under—through lack of money, through a lack of material possessions—but it never happened. I kept after God, letting him know my needs, and he kept me going with the aid of my church—sometimes with the aid of strangers. I lived one day at a time.

Many thoughts come to my mind about Mary. Two of the hardest ones are these: why did Mary's marriage fall apart, and what happened as a result of her telling God she wanted to serve him? I cannot answer the first question, but the second one I can.

I have a newspaper clipping which features Mary: it tells of her efforts a few years ago to raise support worth thousands of pounds in aid of victims of a severe drought in Africa. When I asked her how she managed to find the money and a vehicle to deliver food, tools and the other items that came pouring in, she pointed out that since God proved he was able to meet her material needs after her marriage failed, he could be depended upon to meet other human needs under any circumstances.

I prayed for the lorry first. When a man phoned me and said he had heard I was looking for one and that I may have his, I began to pray for the goods to load it with. Our local newspaper picked up the story, and in a week or so I had thousands of pounds' worth of food and materials to give away.

Today, without the benefit of a steady income, Mary travels back and forth to Africa supervising various projects that help villages improve their living standards.

This is only one of many similar testimonials. Seek out older Christians whom you know and trust. Ask them about their experiences—I'm sure many will tell of heart-breaking failures. Yet it is very likely that nearly all will say Jesus kept his promise: 'I shall never forsake you nor abandon you'. Learn from the experiences of others that you might be better equipped to cope with your own failures. Learn how to help those who are struggling through times of despair.

## The Myth Of The Messiah Complex

Christ is the Lamb of God who takes away the sins of the world. His will is to teach us to reflect glory back to the Father—no matter how high the cost. Christ's agony in the Garden is beyond our comprehension.

Psychiatrists have coined the term 'messiah complex' to describe the condition of certain people who actually desire to fail or suffer. This is a distorted understanding of the character of Christ. In fact Christ requested that God 'Please take away this cup of horror from me'—because nobody in his right mind *desires* to suffer. However, the object lesson for us comes in Jesus' very next breath, 'But I want your will, not mine' (Luke 22:42).

Christians must face the realities of this life honestly, knowing that they will have both good and bad experiences. It is our joy to thank God for the former and our role to trust God when the latter engulf us. It must be conceded to the secular world, however, that if Christ's mission ended on the Cross, then we would be fools not to adopt practical existentialism or profound scepticism, as do so many today. As Paul writes to the church in Corinth, if there is to be no reward of eternal life to come, then 'we apostles are all liars because we have said that God raised Christ from the grave … and if being a Christian is of value to us only now in this life, we are the most miserable of creatures' (I Cor 15:15, 19).

## The Hills Are Alive

The central theme of this chapter is that once God begins a good work in us, he keeps nurturing the seeds of his work—despite all outward appearances of failure.

Julie Andrews, who portrayed the late Maria Von Trapp in the film based on Rodgers and Hammerstein's famous West End musical, *The Sound of Music*, sings, 'I have confidence in confidence.' Well that might be for the West End, but the *real* Maria Von Trapp would have sung different lyrics, ones far more in tune with Paul's words which proclaim confidence in Christ.

When a person becomes a noted celebrity, as Maria Augusta Von Trapp did, it is easy to discount all the suffering that came before (and after) that person's rise to fame. It is quite possible to overlook the shame and the anguish Maria Augusta, then a novice nun awaiting entrance into the holy Order of Saint Benedict, felt the day the Mother Abbess dismissed the young woman from the convent. In her book, *The*

*Trapp Family Singers*, Maria Von Trapp tells of her bitter disappointment:

> 'Tell me, Maria, which is the most important lesson our old Nonnberg has taught you?'
>
> Without a moment's hesitation I answered, looking fully into the beautiful, dark eyes: 'The only important thing on earth for us is to find out what is the will of God and to do it.'
>
> 'Even if it is not pleasant, or if it is hard, perhaps very hard?' The hands tightened on mine.
>
> Well now, she means leaving the world and giving up everything, I thought to myself.
>
> 'Yes, Reverend Mother, even then, and whole-heartedly, too.'
>
> Releasing my hands, Reverend Mother sat back in her chair. 'All right, then, Maria, it seems to be the will of God that you leave us— for a while only,' she continued hastily when she saw my speechless horror.
>
> 'L-l-leave Nonnberg,' I stuttered, and tears welled up in my eyes. I couldn't help it. The motherly woman was very near now, her arms around my shoulders, which were shaking with sobs.'[4]

The novice had two choices following the news that she had failed as a nun. She could have held this against God, who she believed had led her to Nonnberg. Or, she could trust that while this was a painful blow, she would accept it as God's will, knowing that the good work he had started in her was about to flower into full bloom in whatever adventure lay ahead. Maria did the latter:

> I knelt down. The fine, delicately small hand made the Sign of the Cross on my forehead. I kissed the ring and, as through a veil, I had a last

glance into those unforgettable eyes, which seemed to know all about sorrow and suffering, but also victory and peace. I couldn't utter a single word.[5]

The story of how Maria Augusta came to meet the lonely Baron Von Trapp is well known. It is nearly the stuff of fairy tales. Only were it a tale by Hans Andersen, it would have ended when Maria married the Baron and they would have lived happily ever after. Instead, in a very short time Adolf Hitler set off the events which led to World War II. The once wealthy Von Trapps escaped from war-torn Europe with little more than the clothing on their backs. They landed in a big, strange land—the United States—with no money, no jobs and nowhere to live.

Through the help of an acquaintance, the Von Trapps managed to acquire a derelict farmhouse in Vermont, where in time they set up a small maple-syrup business, using the maple trees on the property. After some repairs and building on the property, they were set for a new chapter in their lives.

Considering the great losses the Von Trapps suffered, both materially (the Baron's assets were lost and his palace was confiscated by the Nazis to be used as an administrative centre) and emotionally, one could suppose that this family of Austrians would lose faith in the goodness of a God who would allow them to pass through such trials. Rather, their actions help us to determine how this family of refugees viewed the goodness of their God. Maria tells the story:

All we needed now to complete our happiness was a decent place to worship … we couldn't think of building one now; but next to the old horse barn was the newest building on our

place, a chicken coop, uninhabited. After a lot
of scrubbing and whitewashing, it looked and
smelled clean, and the walls were covered with
thick curtains. Georg made an altar and Maria
made a tabernacle; we put two benches along
the side, and carpets on the floor, and then we
approached our bishop for permission to
reserve the Blessed Eucharist. The permission
was given, and the Feast of Corpus Christi was
celebrated in joy and glory on our hilltop.[6]

One is led to draw a natural parallel between the
first Noel, when our Lord was born in a stable, and
this Mass, which was celebrated in a hen house! The
vision conjured up by the humble conditions of each
setting speaks volumes about God's love for us—
regardless of outward appearances. Maria goes on to
describe times following this celebration:

As the weeks, the months, the years go by, we
see more and more that only one thing is necessary to be happy and to make others
happy, and that one thing is not money, nor
connections, nor health—it is Love.[7]

When God begins a good work he does not stop
until it is finished. Maria Von Trapp never stopped
trusting that God loved her. She accepted the unexpected and allowed God to finish the good work on
the family farm in Vermont. Whatever our failures
and hurts, because he loves us God offers us the Comforter, his Holy Spirit, which I am sure he wishes
every man, woman and child would accept—a blessing available to every Christian.

Maria Von Trapp's comment about God's love
prompts me to add one thought: God asks much of us,
but he gives much in return. He is what Leslie D.

Weatherhead called 'absolute demand and ultimate succour.' The one whom we call Father is liable to ask anything of us, most importantly that we give up ourselves for his sake. Whether or not we do this , the fact still remains that God has already given us everything, most significantly *himself* on Calvary. The one thing the Lord will not do is force us to choose him: it is up to us to make a decision. He may soften our hardened hearts, but we have the ultimate choice.

At the risk of degenerating from the sublime to the ridiculous, I want to share the last verse of a poem which my wife copied out for me a few years ago at a time when rejection slips were landing daily on our doorstep. I was being turned down for jobs which I was fully qualified to do, and what really hurt me was that I was being rejected without even the courtesy of an interview:

> Keep coming back, and though the world may
>    romp across your spine,
> Let every game's end find you still upon the
>    battling line;
> For when the One Great Scorer comes to mark
>    against your name,
> He writes—not that you won or lost—but how
>    you played the game.[8]

In the end of our lives, our actions on earth do matter. What's more, the quality of one's life does not depend on success or failure, because God is interested solely in how we live our lives. I must say how much the poem cheered me when I was feeling like a failure. More encouraging still are Paul's words (Heb 12:1 [RSV]) which also use athletic terms to drive home the same point about the Christian life:

> Therefore, since we are surrounded by so great a cloud of witnesses, let us also lay aside every weight, and sin which clings so closely, and let us run with perseverance the race that is set before us.

In the next line Paul tells us to keep our eyes on Christ for encouragement when we become weary and discouraged with the rigours of this life: 'He was willing to die a shameful death on the Cross because of the joy he knew would be his afterwards; and now he sits in the place of honour by the throne of God' (Heb 12:2).

### 'Arglwydd Arwain Trwy'r Anialwch'

To draw this chapter to a close, I quote a powerful Welsh hymn which, when we analyse its meaning, sums up the message of the last four chapters:

> Guide me, O thou great Redeemer,
>     Pilgrim through this barren land;
> I am weak, but thou art mighty;
>     Hold me with thy powerful hand:
>     Bread of heaven,
> Feed me now and evermore.

It isn't that this earth is barren in a material sense: this world proffers desirable tangible treasures. Earth is barren only in a spiritual sense. If we strive only for the material, we deprive ourselves of the spiritual treasures which may be ours. Only when we call on God to guide us, can we rightly expect to have the proper combination of the physical and spiritual treasures that are necessary for a balanced Christian life. Thus we are fed with the Bread of heaven, like the manna God gave his followers as they wandered in the desert. The manna sustained the daily needs of the

Israelites. That we are in need of healing is evidence that we are subject to serious blows and wounds. To expect to come through this life unscathed because we are Christians is naïve and misguided. Our joy is that in Christ's Holy Spirit, the Comforter, we have a 'crystal fountain' which will heal us—to quote further from the hymn:

> Open now the crystal fountain
> Whence the healing stream doth flow.

It is a fact that the closer we get to God—that is, 'tread[ing] the verge of Jordan'—the more Satan steps up his attacks against us. More from the hymn:

> When I tread the verge of Jordan,
> Bid my anxious fears subside.

Moving from the hymn to an example from CS Lewis, in *The Screwtape Letters*, the senior devil, Screwtape, learns with alarm that the human which his satanic nephew, Wormwood, is bedevilling, has made a renewed profession of faith. Lewis' dry humour makes it easy to miss the point. Screwtape writes:

> It remains to consider how we can retrieve this disaster. The great thing is to prevent his doing anything. As long as he does not convert it into action, it does not matter how much he thinks about his new repentance. Let the little brute wallow in it. Let him, if he has any bent that way, write a book about it; that is often an excellent way of sterilising the seeds which the Enemy [God] plants in a human soul. Let him do anything but act.[9]

Turning back to the Welsh hymn, we see that it

offers us assurance that despite clever subtle attacks, hell's power over all Christians ended on the first Easter:

> Death of death, and hell's destruction,
> Land me safe on Canaan's side.

And so we are able to know with conviction that in spite of all outward appearance of failure, when we pick up our cross and carry it in our Lord's footsteps, we are able to say in faith:

> Songs and praises
> I will ever give to thee.[10]

Remember, the Christian life is made up of good and bad experiences. Based only on limited human observation, it is wrong to assume that we have failed 'until his task within you is finally finished on that day when Jesus Christ returns' (Phil 1:6). In all things God is working out his will in the lives of his children. In the meantime, God speaks to us through good times and bad, when we succeed and when we fail. What matters is to listen to him, to let ourselves be guided by the Spirit, to face up to the adventure God calls us to, despite the risks involved along the way. Let our motto be, 'not my will, but yours, God.' This isn't a fatalistic abandonment of our lives to chance; it is a trusting response to a loving God as demonstrated by Christ himself.

## Notes

[1]John Boykin, *Circumstances and the Role of God* (Zondervan: Michigan, USA, 1986).
[2]David Prior, *The Suffering and the Glory* (Hodder & Stoughton: London, 1985), p 194.

[3]*ibid*.
[4]Maria Augusta Trapp, *The Trapp Family Singers* (Geoffrey Bles: London, 1954), pp 14–15.
[5]*ibid* p 14.
[6]*ibid* pp 223–24.
[7]*ibid* p 287.
[8]Grantland Rice, 'Alumnus Football', *Werner's Readings and Recitations*, no 54 (1915), p 167.
[9]CS Lewis, *The Screwtape Letters* (Geoffrey Bles: London, 1946), pp 69–70.
[10]*Hymns Ancient & Modern Revised* (William Clowes & Sons, Ltd: London), p 238.

# Chapter 5

# The Origins Of Failure

## On Pessimism, Adam And El Dorado

For centuries, men and women have been inventing myths and philosophies in order to cope with pain, failure and mortality.

The ancient Greeks knew that thanks to the inquisitiveness of Pandora, all manner of evil maladies were unleashed on humanity. Two popular ways for the Greek to cope with his troubles were Epicureanism, the philosophy of 'eat, drink and be merry today, for tomorrow you die'; and Stoicism, the philosophy of enduring all pain and discomfort with a passive acceptance.

Despite their pessimistic realism, embedded deeply in the collective consciousness of the Greek mind was a niggling longing for the pre-Pandora paradise on earth—that which Homer called the 'Golden Age', when failure did not exist and there was peace on earth.

The Greeks were not alone in their attempts at finding meaning in life's short, turbulent existence. In the ancient Hebrew way of thinking, it was Adam's fall that forced men to earn their living by tilling the cursed soil all the days of their lives. As a result, a pessimistic philosophy springs forth from the dour writer of Ecclesiastes. Commenting on the utter futility of life, the author writes:

> I, the Preacher, was king of Israel, living in Jerusalem. And I applied myself to search for understanding about everything in the universe. I discovered that the lot of man, which God has

dealt him, is not a happy one. It is all foolish-
ness, chasing the wind. What is wrong cannot be
righted; it is water over the dam; and there is no
use thinking of what might have been.

(Eccl 1:12–15)

Centuries later, as Christianity spread throughout
the Mediterranean regions, acute pessimism gave way
to a fresh optimism owing to the promise of new life in
the future resurrection. The evangelist Nigel Lee,
speaking at a conference sponsored by the Oxford
University Christian Union, points out that before the
Christian era, ancient sarcophagi reflected the
gloomiest epitaphs lamenting the loss of life: 'I was
once as you are now—enjoying cups of wine and
plates of meat; now I am wine and meat for worms.'
But after the dawn of the Christian era, the epitaphs
proclaimed optimistically, 'Dead to the world—alive
with the Lord!'

At last men and women could be assured of a better
life to come, by virtue of believing in the name of
Jesus Christ. Admittedly, amongst many pagan relig-
ions, there was a promised afterlife, but this place was
usually reserved for the valiant and the worthy only:
on the whole, women, children, the infirm, the weak,
slaves—indeed the *failures* of these cultures in terms
of pagan values—were not offered a place in the afterlife. The Christian knew the next life was neither
annihilation nor an unknowable mystery, and not a
prize awarded for success or good works. Thus the
message of salvation through Christ came to be called
the 'Good News'. It must be added, however, that
while the Christian message was broadly preached
and many lives were affected by the Good News,
human suffering, pain and death remained too great a
problem to be smoothed over with only a veneer of

Christian doctrine or 'unrealistic' hopes. So despite the offer of a new life in Christ, the majority of people lived on in pessimism.

In modern times, when Columbus found (from the European point of view) a 'new world', there grew up rumours of an unspoilt land where there was plenty for all. Soon Spanish sailors talked of the pleasures of El Dorado, a resplendent city of gold where everyone would be rich and there would be no want or pain. There was also supposed to be a fountain of youth, in what is now Florida, which would make people immortal. (Some modern land developers still think it's there, I imagine!) People began to long for the unlimited pleasures one could enjoy: to be immortal in a land free from pain and death.

We ought not to scoff at these longings. Many of our modern university courses on social welfare teach that humanity is perfectible; politicians vainly promise increased social benefits, more jobs and, of course, all this with lower taxes. Television, the cinema and the theatre offer us an increasing menu of escapist entertainment. Not least, the market place is filled with all sorts of health aids that glibly promise to make us lose weight without dieting, replace lost hair or make us irresistible to the opposite sex. This is merely the age-old attempt at coping with a life of fleeting joys, much pain and the ultimate failure—mortality. As the sombre preacher in Ecclesiastes moans, 'there is nothing new under the sun' (Eccl 1:9 [RSV]).

## Why Did God Make Life So Difficult?

One possible conclusion we may draw from humanity's deep dissatisfaction with life may be that something has gone terribly wrong in the world. Maybe things aren't the way they were originally intended by

God. Let's explore this possibility as a means of helping us to understand more about why Christians fail. To do this, we must consider Adam and Eve.

## Adam And Eve And Pinch Me...

When I began writing this book, I intended to eschew all references to Adam and Eve because so many people have trivialised this part of Genesis which tells of the origins of the human race. I thought of the old children's rhyme:

> Adam and Eve and Pinch Me
>   went down to the sea to bathe;
> Adam and Eve was drowned—
>   who do you think was saved?
> Pinch Me.

There is no denying that for many, Adam and Eve are not to be taken seriously. After all, science and Darwin's theory proclaim that humanity evolved from lower life forms, and therefore Adam and Eve belong in the same category as Pandora, El Dorado and the rest of the world's mythology. Ironically, Darwin did not intend to debunk Adam and Eve. In fact, when asked by Tennyson whether his theory was an attack on Christianity in general, Darwin retorted, 'No, certainly not'.[1] Yet, contrary to the personal opinions of Darwin, what the theory behind *The Origin of Species* 'indicated, if consistently adopted, [was] the pithecoid origin of the human race.'[2]

## The Myth Of Popular Science?

A popular scientific theory teaches that, put on a graph, humanity is continuing on an upward rise from obscurity, nearing perfection with each succeeding age. In a condensed version of this theory, life could have begun in a murky pool of water which was struck by lightning, and since then we have been evolving in an unbroken chain towards perfection. The typical illustration one might find in any school book is of a parade of hairy bipeds beginning on the left with a crouching creature and ending on the right with an erect *Homo sapiens* striding boldly towards perfection. One may call this a scientific myth because, as with any myth, this cannot be proved or disproved.

### The Myth Of The Bible?

According to the account we have in our Bibles, we see that humanity was created in a perfect state and was originally designed to live for ever in harmony with the rest of creation. However, if we drew a graph, we would see that according to the Bible, humanity is on a downward road, which after a life of pain and sorrow, terminates in death. Thus humanity carries to the grave the collective remembrance of a paradise lost.

Whichever theory we subscribe to—Darwin's or the Bible's—each one requires some amount of faith to believe. Moreover, no matter what we believe about humanity, the one thing which remains unchanged is that, as humans, we are currently imperfect.

It isn't my purpose to try to prove or disprove the existence of a literal Adam and Eve. Having said this, the story of the Fall in the Garden of Eden must be considered if we are going to explore why God allows Christians to fail. For, whether they are literally or figuratively true, Adam and Eve can be seen as the world's first failures.

## The Apostle Paul On Adam

Paul alludes to Adam and Eve in the forum at Mars Hill in Athens where he attempts to utilise the Greeks' liberal-mindedness to teach them about Jesus. In addition to their own pantheon of gods, they had a shrine to one called simply 'The Unknown God'. Paul points out to the Athenians:

> You have been worshipping [The Unknown God] ... without knowing who he is, and now I wish to tell you about him. He made the world and everything in it, and since he is Lord of heaven and earth, he doesn't live in man-made temples; and human hands can't minister to his needs—for he has no needs!   (Acts 17:23–25)

Here we see Paul the iconoclast. He runs the risk of insulting the Greeks by sticking a pin in one of their time-honoured myths: that their gods actually dwell in mortar and stone abodes. Since Paul is debunking myths, what he says next suggests that, in his estimation at least, Adam and Eve were not of the same ilk as, say, Artemis or Apollo: 'He [God] ... gives life and breath to everything, and satisfies every need there is. He created all the people of the world from one man, Adam, and scattered the nations across the face of the earth' (Acts 17:25–26).

## The Origin Of Failure

In his letter to the church in Rome, Paul identifies the origins of all human failure: 'When Adam sinned, sin entered the entire human race. His sin spread death throughout all the world, so everything began to grow old and die, for all sinned' (Rom 5:12). The origin of failure, then, stems from separation from God through *sin*.

## Failure: The Risk Of Free Will

Eve and then Adam ate a piece of fruit. They really ought not to have eaten it, but they did. Yet, is that any reason to slam the gates of Eden in their faces, turning them out into a cursed land to endure harsh failure? (Gen 3:17–19) What parent would react so strongly if a child disobeyed what seemed to be a minor domestic rule?

It is best to examine carefully the facts of this case before we attempt to answer these questions. According to Genesis 2, Eve and Adam were quite content with their relationship with God and obeyed his wish that they refrain from eating the fruit of a certain tree in the centre of the Garden.

At the start of Genesis 3, however, a snake (Satan) creeps into the Garden and attempts to confuse Eve:

> 'Really?' he asked, '*None* of the fruit in the Garden? God says you mustn't eat *any* of it?' [They may eat of all the fruit except one.] ...'God says we mustn't eat it or even touch it, or we will die.'
> 'That's a lie!' the serpent hissed. 'You'll not die! God knows very well that the instant you eat it you will become like him, for your eyes will be opened—you will be able to distinguish good from evil.'                    (Gen 3:1–5)

Satan, the original liar, mixes in some truth to muddle Eve's thinking: his lie is that they will not die; the truth is that they will have their eyes open to awesome knowledge. Satan has planted doubts in Eve's mind. Eve has to exercise her will at this point. Listening to what a total stranger has said, she has to decide if God, whom she knows intimately , is trustworthy. Imagine a smooth-talking stranger telling you that your grandfather was actually a Nazi war criminal. Would you believe it? Eve chose to believe the worst about God. Satan's tempting morsel caused her to doubt God's veracity, and to feel dissatisfied with her lot. She desired for the first time to be equal to God—to be 'like him'.

Fanning the flames of pride is Satan's speciality. While it is not explicit in Scripture, this is probably the same sin which caused Satan to fall from heaven (Rev 7—9; Luke 10:18). Ever since then, Satan has been working to overthrow God's purposes in the universe by enticing His creatures to become saboteurs.

Eve covets God's knowledge and power; she begins to feel pride at the prospect of gaining new knowledge and self-sufficiency. The Greek considered *hubris*—pride—to be the deadliest of all personal sins. The Hebrew Proverb teaches, 'Pride goes before destruction and haughtiness before a fall' (Prov 16:18).

Satan held his breath, watching with expectancy to see if his victim would disobey God of her own free will. The Evil One knew that—odious as dissatisfaction and pride are—they are merely *potential* sin in the form of temptation.

Temptation alone is not sin. To illustrate this point, I'll tell you about a friend of mine called Tom. He and his wife once found some *Penthouse Magazines* under their son Gary's mattress while they were changing the bedding. They were very embarrassed by the explicit and lewd pictures. Removing the material, Tom decided to wait for the right moment to talk to their son about the magazines.

After dinner Tom invited his son into his study for a cup of coffee. After chatting a while, my friend gently confronted Gary, confessing that he and his wife had accidentally found the magazines. There was an awkward pause. Then Tom explained, 'Gary, your mother and I strongly disapprove of the way sex is depicted in these magazines. I think you know why.' The teenager nodded sullenly. 'To demonstrate our disapproval, I have no choice but to punish you for buying these.' What Tom said next drives home an important point about sin as opposed to just temptation. He added quickly, 'Before I send you to your room, Gary, I want you to know something else. After I found the magazines, I came down here to think what I was going to do about it.'

The boy nodded, now hardly meeting his father's eye.

Reaching out and touching Gary's shoulder, he swallowed hard and said, 'I want you to know I was very tempted to close the door and sit in here and enjoy looking at these pictures, myself.'

The boy glanced up sharply and looked in wonder at his father who continued, adding, 'There is nothing wrong with having an appetite for sex—I enjoy making love to your mother—but this stuff is degrading not only to the men and women who posed for the photos, but it degrades a wonderful gift given to us by God—the gift of intimate sexuality. God understands our appetites, but he also expects us to be strong enough to stand firm when they tempt us to sin. It isn't easy, I know—but I wanted to show you it can be done.'

'Resist the devil and he will flee from you,' advises James 4:7. Likewise, Peter warns that Satan is always waiting to pounce on us, so we must 'Stand firm when he attacks' (I Peter 5:9).

According to the account in Genesis (Gen 3:1–6), after Eve heard Satan's lie, instead of resisting, or turning away, 'The woman was convinced. How lovely and fresh looking it was! And it would make her so wise! So she ate some of the fruit' (Gen 3:6). Eve exercised free will and the result was disastrous failure.

## God Created Sin?

A few years ago I was commuting back and forth to work near Philadelphia, USA. One day I saw some graffiti painted in broad white strokes on a wall by the side of the road. It read: *God Created Deseas* (sic). I smiled at the spelling and promptly forgot about it. The next morning as I drove to work, I saw that someone else had taken white paint and below the first message had added the words, *An' all de fishes in dem*.

Ignoring the Philadelphia accents, the idea that God created disease and therefore sin, failure, suffering and death is misguided. Why?—Adam and Eve willingly ate the fruit:

> And as they ate it, suddenly they became aware of their nakedness, and were embarrassed. So they strung fig leaves together to cover themselves around the hips.
>
> That evening they heard the sound of the Lord God walking in the Garden; and they hid themselves among the trees. The Lord God called to Adam, 'Why are you hiding?'
>
> And Adam replied, 'I heard you coming and didn't want you to see me naked. So I hid.'
>
> 'Who told you you were naked?' the Lord God asked. 'Have you eaten fruit from the tree I warned you about?'
>
> 'Yes,' Adam admitted 'but it was the woman *you* gave me who brought me some, and I ate it.'
>
> (Gen 3:7–12. Emphasis mine)

Adam tries to place the blame for his sin on God, as if the Lord was responsible for their abusing the gift of free will and the inevitable introduction of pain and death into the human realm. Adam was the first of many to hurl this accusation at God. However, the truth is that mortification, failure and separation from God (spiritual death) exist because of the wickedness which lies in the human heart.[3]

The prophet Isaiah knew the wickedness of the human heart when he wrote this telling passage which underscores our wickedness and our reluctance to repent:

> We despised him and rejected him—a man of sorrows, acquainted with bitterest grief. We turned our backs on him and looked the other way when he went by. He was despised and we didn't care.
>     Yet it was *our* grief he bore, *our* sorrows that weighed him down.          (Isa 53:3–4)

### Did Adam's Sin Cause Natural Disasters?

Many people wonder why God allows failure, pain and even death to result from natural disasters such as famine, earthquake and drought. God said,

> Because you listened to the voice of your wife, and have eaten of the tree of which I commanded you, 'You shall not eat of it,' cursed is the ground because of you; in toil you shall eat of it all the days of your life; thorns and thistles it shall bring forth to you.   (Gen 3:17–18 [RSV])

The Judaeo-Christian explanation of how every sort of evil entered into the world, including natural disasters, may be traced back to Adam's and Eve's sin. Their tenure in Paradise depended upon their desire to obey God's mandate not to eat the fruit. Adam and Eve chose to disregard God's warning and thus the first failure of humanity resulted. It was not the temptation, but the *succumbing* to that temptation which was the sin. Wilful disobedience brought both spiritual and physical death into history.[4] None of this was God's intention, but Adam and Eve gained the forbidden knowledge of good and evil which meant from then on, they and their offspring were culpable.

It is important to remember that in his infinite mercy, despite this terrible turn of events at the dawn of human history, God provided a way out for humanity. Paul encourages us when he proclaims that we are not to be fearful in our failure-prone universe. He says with joy and authority:

> For all who are led by the Spirit of God are sons of God.
> And so we should not be like cringing, fearful slaves, but we should behave like God's very own children.... And since we are his children, we will share his treasures—for all God gives to his son Jesus is now ours too. But if we are to share his glory, we must also share his suffering.
> Yet what we suffer now is nothing compared to the glory he will give us later. For all creation is waiting patiently and hopefully for that future day when God will resurrect his children. For on that day thorns and thistles, sin, death, and [failure] ... —the things that overcame the world ... will all disappear, and the world around us will share in the glorious freedom from sin which God's children enjoy.
> For we know that even the things of nature, like animals and plants, suffer in sickness and death [the cursed earth] as they await this great event. And even we Christians, although we have the Holy Spirit within us as a foretaste of future glory, also groan to be released from pain and suffering.          (Rom 8:14–15, 17–23)

### Jesus—The One And Only Great Second Chance

If the Bible spoke only about the origins and effects of

human misery, then this Adamic theory would be no better than the story of Pandora. However, the Bible formulates an exceedingly important doctrine, using the sin of Adam as the kernel of the argument. Paul declares:

> What a contrast between Adam and Christ who was yet to come! And what a difference between man's sin and God's forgiveness!
> For this one man, Adam, brought death to many through his *sin*. But this one man, Jesus Christ, brought forgiveness to many through God's *mercy*. Adam's *one* sin brought the penalty of death to many, while Christ freely takes away *many* sins and gives glorious life instead.
>
> (Romans 5:14–16)

Earlier, I mentioned that I was tempted to avoid any references to Adam and Eve. Yet Paul mentions the name of Adam again and again in his discourse. Whether or not Paul believed in a literal Adam and Eve is a moot point here. However, two things are clear from these crucial passages of Scripture which mention Adam: first, the account of the Fall is of central importance to Christian doctrine as it relates to why Christians fail; second, although we will continue to fail—often times dismally—there is reason to be optimistic because of the hope offered to us through Christ.

## God Weeps

What may we conclude, then? As did Jesus Christ, we all must endure failures that leave us scarred. But when we are scarred by failure in our attempts to serve God, we must never forget that Jesus stands with us in every trial. When we weep, so he weeps:

Only twice in the Gospels is it recorded that our
Lord wept, for only the most intense grief could
have wrung tears from so strong a man. He wept
at the grave of Lazarus over the grief of the
world and the hatefulness of death, and he wept
... over the terror and agony of war and destruction; and we can believe that he wept not only
over this particular war that would destroy the
beloved city of Jerusalem, but over the passion
of the whole world until the end of time. 'For
nation will rise up against nation, and kingdom
against kingdom,' he said to his disciples, 'and
there shall be famines, and pestilences, and
earthquakes.... All of these are the beginnings
of sorrows.... And because iniquity shall
abound, the love of many shall wax cold.' God
has given man the gift of free will, and without
destroying our manhood, he cannot take it back
again to save us from the results of what we have
chosen. Choosing sin, we choose also grief and
war and death; but while we endure what we
have chosen, we can remember that God
weeps.[5]

## Looking Ahead

In the next two chapters, it will be my aim to establish
how God has shown himself to be in complete control
of events which in the eyes of a pessimistic world
appear to be colossal failures. We will look at the lives
of Moses and Peter, examining under the microscope
their blemishes and weaknesses. My aim is not to set
about proving the obvious—that human beings will
fail from time to time. Rather, it is my hope to show
how God may use our failures to bring about his ultimate plan if we allow him to. This, after all, is the
essence of all Christian hope and faith: that all things
are working together towards the consummation of the

universe in the victorious return of Jesus Christ. Thus
to Julïan of Norwich God revealed these words: 'See, I
am God; see, I am in all things.... See, I lift never
mine hands off my work, nor ever shall, without end.'[6]

## Notes

[1] Bernard MG Reardon, *From Coleridge to Gore: A
Century of Religious Thought in Britain* (Longman
Group Ltd: London, 1971), p 292.
[2] *ibid.*
[3] Many people believe that the disease AIDS is God's
punishment on permissive heterosexuals and
homosexuals. This is nonsense, for it is not God's way
in this age of grace, to inflict physical punishment on
sinners. If it were, which of us would be spared? AIDS
and other sexually transmitted diseases are the consequence of man's gross disobedience of God's warning to remain chaste, or to limit sexual activity to a
monogamous, heterosexual relationship. Rather than
blame God who warned us about the results of sexual
gluttony, we may place the blame on our sexual revolution. Ironically, governments are passing out
pamphlets warning us to curb our sexual practices as a
way to remain healthy, ignoring the fact the Bible has
been doing so for centuries.
[4] Adam and Eve understood that they may stay in the
Garden as long as they obeyed God's explicit command not to eat a certain fruit. God warned Adam of
the consequences of disobedience. The result of their
wilful act of disobedience led to two results: (a)
spiritual death, by which human nature was corrupted
and became separated from the Creator; (b) physical
death: according to Paul, physical death is the price
we all must pay because of sin (Rom 6:23). While it
does not state in the Bible that humans were originally

immortal, Theodore Vriezen states,

> that man was originally placed in Paradise near
> the tree of life, without being forbidden to eat
> its fruit. In other words Genesis 2 f states that
> according to the will of God, man was initially
> granted the possibility of eternal life by means
> of the fruit of the tree of life.
>
> (Theodore C Vriezen, *An Outline of Old
> Testament Theology* [Blackwell & Mott:
> Oxford, 1958], p 205)

Furthermore, the doctrine of original sin states that all
of Adam's descendents suffer the results of spiritual
and physical death. Many people will not accept the
fact that we must suffer because of Adam's sin. Paul
tells us we know it was Adam's sin which caused
death:

> Therefore as sin came into the world through
> one man [Adam] and death through sin, and so
> death spread to all men because all men sin-
> ned—sin indeed was in the world before the law
> was given, but sin is not counted where there is
> no law. Yet death reigned from Adam to
> Moses, even over those whose sins were not like
> the transgression of Adam, who was a type of
> the one who was to come.
>
> (Rom 5:12–14 [RSV])

Paul goes on to say, 'For if many died through one
man's trespass, much more have the grace of God and
the free gift in the grace of that one man Jesus Christ
abounded for many' (Rom 5:15 [RSV]).
⁵Elizabeth Goudge, *God So Loved the World* (Hodder & Stoughton Ltd: London, 1961), pp 208–209.
⁶Maria Boulding, *Gateway to Hope* (Fount: London,
1985), p 148.

## Chapter 6
# The Fugitive

A young man sees a member of his own downtrodden group being beaten up by a hated rival. In a frenzy, he searches through his own cloak, but still keeps his alert dark eyes on the scene. After what seems like an agonisingly long moment, his searching fingers find what they are looking for. His shaking hand flies into the air, and there is a blinding silver flash against the cloudless blue sky, the sun's rays reflecting off the hilt of a well-honed dagger. Next comes the rip of splitting threads and the sickening tear of parting human flesh.

There is an astonished groan: the limp body slumps with its full weight to the ground and twitches while a pool of blood seeps into the cracks of the dry earth.

'Run! He'll never raise his hand against any of us again,' cries the young man. Gazing around him when the boy he has rescued has gone, he makes certain no one else has seen his deed. Wiping the wet dagger on the dead man's sleeve, the young man sheathes the weapon, then hides the body quickly. For now, he walks away calmly. Yet less than 24 hours later, he is a fugitive from the law, running for his life. Behind him he leaves his family, his friends and everything he had ever worked for.

Is this a scene from an old James Dean film? Perhaps it's a scene from the revolving stage of Stratford-on-Avon, and Romeo is on his way to his only friend, Friar Laurence, for safe-keeping?

Actually, this is the young Moses, and the story may be read in Exodus.

If you have read either Charles Colson's book, *Born Again*,[1] or Rita Nightingale's *Freed for Life*,[2] you will agree that the lowest caste in the world, the individual most likely to have the indelible word *failure* stamped on his forehead, is the criminal.

Recently, a chance routine check showed that a senior social worker in the North of England had falsified some information on his original job application years earlier. He had not only falsified his name and age, but it turned out that he had once been convicted of child molesting and had served a prison sentence. In a matter of one day, the new life he had worked to establish ended—including his new identity as a respected family man—and he was dismissed from his post because he had once been an outlaw.

Although I do not condone his lying, I can understand why this person tried to hide the facts about his past. Once someone has been a criminal, either he must live with that stigma for life—or try by whatever means possible to run from his past. One of several reasons why few men and women are truly reformed after having been criminals is because society will not believe they have been reformed. Criminals in fact are perceived as permanent social failures. In his autbiography, *Killing Time*[3], Noel Fellowes—a man accused and imprisoned unjustly for manslaughter—experiences these problems acutely after being released from prison. His life is now a testimony to God's goodness, but he feels no less strongly the injustices that were inflicted upon him both during his prison sentence and afterwards as he tried desperately to build a new life against all the odds society mercilessly threw at him.

### And God Came In

Moses was a criminal. He made his way into the only place left for him to go: the desert. Keeping the facts about his crime obscure, he began a new life in the far-off land of Midian. There, this adopted grandson of the all-powerful Egyptian Pharaoh assumed the comparatively demeaning role of looking after the flocks of a priest named Jethro. Yet this was a man once destined to live a life of royal distinction.

The life of a shepherd is an introspective one, and Moses would have had plenty of time to reflect on his past. Thinking about his crime, he would have seen that while his intention was good—he was protecting a helpless Hebrew slave from the whip of an Egyptian slave master—his method wasn't. Moses was placing himself above the law of the land.

One day his wanderings brought him and his sheep to the mountain of Horeb, or Mount Sinai.

'If only I hadn't killed that man,' he might have said bitterly through gritted teeth. (He wouldn't have worried who heard since there were only sheep surrounding him.) 'If I hadn't, I could have been able to help my people by using my position in the government. If I return to Egypt now, they'll only kill me.'

Apparently more than just the sheep were listening. No sooner had Moses spoken than he met with the Angel of Jehovah who appeared in the form of a burning bush.

> When Moses saw that the bush was on fire and that it didn't burn up, he went over to investigate. Then God [came into Moses' life, speaking from the flames of the bush]...:
> 'Moses! Moses!'
> 'Who is it?' Moses asked.
> 'Don't come any closer,' God told him. 'Take off your shoes, for you are standing on holy ground. I am the God of your fathers—the God of Abraham, Isaac and Jacob.' (Moses covered

his face with his hands, for he was afraid to look at God.)

Then the Lord told him, 'I have seen the deep sorrows of my people in Egypt, and I have heard their pleas for freedom from their harsh taskmasters. I have come to deliver them from the Egyptians and to take them out of Egypt into a good land, a large land, a land "flowing with milk and honey"—the land where the Canaanites, Hittites, Amorites, Perizzites, Hivites, and Jebusites live. Yes, the wail of the people of Israel has risen to me in heaven, and I have seen the heavy tasks the Egyptians have oppressed them with.'                    (Exod 3:2–9)

No doubt Moses was at once terrified by the mysterious voice, yet at the same time, overjoyed at the good news that at last his people were soon to be delivered. Moses might even have tried to glance at the Glory of God before him, but would have had to resume hiding his eyes from a light brighter than the sun at noon on a July day. As he stood trembling with excitement, Moses wondered how God planned to free the Hebrews, though he did not dare ask—he had too much respect for the Power and the Majesty before him. Knowing his thoughts, though, God answered his question: 'Now I am going to send you to Pharaoh, to demand that he let you lead my people out of Egypt' (Exod 3:10).

Dropping his hands but keeping his eyelids tightly closed, Moses uttered in disbelief, 'But I'm not the person for a job like that!' (Exod 3:11)

### Drawing Straight Lines With Crooked Sticks

Why would God select a man who is branded by society as a failure to undertake so momentous a task? Surely when someone wants an important job done, he selects the best man or woman for the task? If I needed to have an audit done, I would not pick an accountant who appeared incompetent—however, that would be logic induced purely by my propensity to judge on outward appearances. God, on the other hand, does not adopt this unfair tack.

At this point in his life, Moses must have longed to cry out to God either words or a song very similar to those of David, many, many years later:

> Sprinkle me with the cleansing blood and I shall
> be clean again.
> Wash me and I shall be whiter than snow.
> And after you have punished me, give me back
> my joy again.
> Don't keep looking at my sins—erase them
> from your sight.
> Create in me a new, clean heart, O God,
> filled with clean thoughts and right desires.
> Don't toss me aside, banished for ever from
> your presence....
> You don't want penance; if you did, how gladly
> I would do it!
> You aren't interested in offerings burned before
> you on the altar.
> It is a broken spirit you want—remorse and
> penitence. A broken and a contrite heart, O
> God, you will not ignore.
>
> (Psalm 51:7–11; 16–17)

Moses did not know of Jehovah's magnanimity towards sinful failures at that time. He was to learn rapidly. In the meantime, he was faced with the awesome prospect of having to return to Egypt where he was wanted by the law. He wondered what God thought of this:

Then God told him, 'I will certainly be with you,

and this is the proof that I am the one sending
you: when you have led the people out of Egypt,
you shall worship God here upon this moun-
tain!'                                        (Exod 3:12)

Looked at from one point of view, this is rich com-
edy: an outlaw confronted on a barren mountain-top
by a talking bush which—although it is on fire—is
neither hot, nor is it being consumed. What's more,
this bush is telling Moses to go back to the last place on
earth he would dare to go!

Imagine this as a film, with Moses being played by
Woody Allen complete with his bookish horn-rimmed
glasses and Yiddish New York accent: 'They won't
believe me! They won't do what *I* tell them to. They'll
say, "Jehovah never appeared to you!"' (Exod 4:1)

To prove to Moses that he needn't worry, God
promises to do miracles to establish Moses' credibility
in the eyes of the Egyptians. But Moses pleads, 'O
Lord, I'm just not a good speaker. I never have been,
and I'm not now, even after you have spoken to me,
for I have a speech impediment' (Exod 4:10). (I can
hear Woody Allen saying, 'Besides, I can't go back
there—I'm allergic to death!')

As Moses and God stand there arguing, one thing
becomes clear. Moses is not the confident natural
leader of men we often imagine him to be. In fact, the
longer this dialogue goes on, the more unsuited to the
task Moses seems. This drives home the point God
wishes to make to all people everywhere: none of us,
of our own strength alone, is capable of serving God
properly.

Through the entire tradition regarding Moses'
call, appears an attitude which marked this
man's work to a pre-eminent degree. It is that
God is put to the fore as the real doer of what is

done. Moses' 'Who am I?' is met with no assurance that he is the man for the task but only with
the promise: 'Certainly, I will be with thee.'[4]

Commenting on Moses' speech defect, God replies,
'Who makes mouths?' (Exod 4:11). This question is
easily overlooked but merits some attention. One of
the tricks Satan loves to use is based on his understanding of human self-image. Moses' self-abasement
seems to masquerade as humility. But the fact is, it is
only a form of self-pity, and self-pity is the opposite of
genuine humility. Since God is not relying upon
human talent to carry out his work, any who wish to
serve him needn't feel they are inadequate, no matter
what their limitations are. In fact, the more severe the
human limitations, quite often, the more powerfully
they are used by God. We only must be willing to do
God's will—he won't force us. Moses' speech impediment can also be likened to Paul's 'thorn'—a disad-
vantage which served to keep him humble.

## God In You

I can make a small parallel between Moses' feeling of
inadequacy and an experience in my own life. When I
started producing religious programmes for the BBC,
it was on a six-month trial basis. To be honest, I felt
entirely unqualified for the job. First of all, I wasn't
ordained—and second, nearly all of my journalism
experience was non-religious. I began to wish I hadn't
got the job.

When I expressed this view to my wife, Judith, she
criticised me, saying, 'You yourself told God he may
use you however he likes, right?'

I nodded reluctantly because I knew what she was
driving at.

'So your attitude is pretty bad. I think you owe it to

God to assume that if he wants you to have this job with the BBC, then you will be able to do it. You won't be alone—God will be with you, too. In the meantime, if you don't start thinking pretty seriously about what you intend to produce, you'll have nobody but yourself to blame if you do mess things up!'

In the end, I knew my wife was right (as usual) and I was simply looking for excuses which would compensate for the hurt I might feel if I was sacked after my trial period. What was worse, I was acting as if I did not believe that God 'causes [me] ... to walk a steady tread like mountain goats upon the rocks' (II Sam 22:34).

Some Christians say we can't know for certain that God has a plan for our lives. The argument here comes down to this: do we act of our own free will, or are we merely actors playing out roles directed by God? Both theories have strong arguments supporting them.

Some Christians stretch the point as far as to say that God reserves parking places for them—this is clearly nonsense. Yet God tells us in Jeremiah 29:11, 'For I know the plans I have for you.... They are plans for good and not for evil, to give you a future and a hope.' Proverbs 19:21 says, 'Man proposes, but God disposes.' Or as the Revised Standard Version puts it, 'Many are the plans in the mind of a man, but it is the purpose of the Lord that will be established.'

My own conclusion from this is that when we place our lives entirely in Christ's hands, he is fully in control—we are not having our will subordinated. Our will is to do God's will; our desire is for God to be in all we say and do.

Moses was positive he could not accomplish the things God had for him to do. When at last he simply begged God to spare him from such ambitious plans,

God—rather than torture his faithless servant—made a special arrangement to help Moses get started on the right road: the Lord allowed Aaron and Moses to work together, supporting each other. Aaron was to speak, and Moses was to give his brother the words to say (Exod 4:14–16).

## Let My People Go

Travelling back to Egypt with Aaron, Moses was able to convince the Israelites, with the assistance of Aaron, that God had indeed selected him to deliver them all from bondage. This was no mean feat. Most of the people had never heard of Moses, but they recognised God in him and saw they had hope of gaining freedom.

Moses knew he was no longer in danger in Egypt because the reigning Pharaoh was not the same one who reigned when Moses' crime was committed. Moses and Aaron gained an audience with the ruler of Egypt and requested in the name of the God of Israel the freedom of the Israelites (Exod 5:1).

The task of convincing the hard-hearted Pharaoh was not an easy one. Exodus chapters 5 to 12 depict Moses as a man of great patience and skill when it came to dealing with the stubborn whims of the Pharaoh. Moses was finding that the more he trusted God—Jehovah—the more God proved his faithfulness. It came as no surprise when the exasperated Pharaoh eventually submitted by saying, 'Leave us; please go away, all of you; go and serve Jehovah as you said' (Exod 12:31). This was surely, to borrow a phrase from Winston Churchill, Moses' 'finest hour'. Even if there were any among the Hebrews who could recall that Moses was actually a fugitive from the law, they were willing to overlook the fact. Moses became a national hero, and it was a time to celebrate the significant victory in the name of Jehovah. To this day Jews pause to mark the departure of their ancestors from slavery by the feast of the Passover. The feast serves as a reminder of the events surrounding the great Exodus.

## God—The Author Of History

If this story had been a screenplay composed in Hollywood, it would have ended with the Jews marching boldly into the sunset, singing a jubilant hymn as the film's credits rolled across the big screen. The escapism of the cinema is too often a poor reflection of reality. The truth is, Moses' adventures were only just beginning: he was destined for some pretty significant set-backs in the days ahead in the wilderness. The many years Moses had spent tending sheep for Jethro were not wasted. Just as sheep can be fickle, stubborn and stupid, so too were God's chosen people—a band of former slaves—once they reached the Red Sea and discovered that Pharaoh's men were in hot pursuit.

The Israelites seemed to have forgotten they had seen Moses perform miracles, call down plagues from heaven and had also seen a mystical pillar of fire lead them directly to the spot where they now stood, trembling like rabbits. With an almost united voice, they turned on their leader and blamed him for the situation they now faced, crying:

> Have you brought us out here to die because there were not enough graves for us in Egypt? Why did you make us leave Egypt? Isn't this what we told you, while we slaves, to leave us alone? We said it would be better to be slaves to the Egyptians than dead in the wilderness.
>
> (Exod 14:11–12)

How different are we today? Do we have a tendency to forget the times God has helped us through difficult moments? Do we err on the side of pessimism rather than optimism? When the Israelites turned their backs on Moses, I am sure he must have felt the temptation to plunge himself into the sea—it must have looked bleak, and his confidence must have wavered, however momentarily.

If Moses had opted for suicide, this story would be nothing more than profoundly pessimistic. Many modern novels extol this blueprint. Fortunately, the author of history and creator of the universe is not a pessimistic novelist. God offers hope. Though the brightness of Moses' 'finest hour' had tarnished, and though he was about as popular as Winston Churchill following World War II, he had the sense to trust God—regardless of circumstances. Moses said to the people, 'Don't be afraid. Just stand where you are and watch, and you will see the wonderful way the Lord will rescue you today. The Egyptians you are looking at—you will never see them again' (Exod 14:13).

He raised his arms, and God sent the strong east wind which blew all night and caused the Red Sea to part, allowing the Hebrews to escape. When the Egyptians entered into the same dry passageway, the waters returned suddenly, and they drowned (Exod 14:21–28).

## In The Wilderness

Predictably, the Hebrews began to grumble as the food supply ran out and the water was used up. Once again, Moses assured them that though he could not do anything about it, surely God would. The very next morning, and every day for about 40 years thereafter, the Israelites had manna—a white gum like coriander seed and bdellium, with a honey taste—which they found on the ground each morning after the dew had gone.

For the time being, Moses had regained the respect of his people. Yet not long after they entered the wilderness at Rephidim—a wasteland of sand and gravel, with intense heat by day and extreme cold by night—there were more big problems. The people complained, saying, 'Give us water!' In his mind Moses must have wondered why God had promised to make him a great leader, when up until now he had succeeded only in leading his people to the brink of disaster, just to be bailed out by God at the last minute. The people were so annoyed with Moses that some had even threatened to stone him.

As any of us might, Moses may have forgotten the original agreement with God, which stipulated it would not be Moses who would do the leading; God was in control. The reassurance was soon to follow:

> Then Jehovah said to Moses, 'Take the elders of Israel with you and lead the people out to Mount Horeb. I will meet you there at the rock. Strike it with your rod—the same one you struck the Nile with—and water will come pouring out, enough for everyone!' Moses did as he was told, and the water gushed out.
>
> (Exod 17:5–6)

### Deus Ex Machina?

It may seem as if all Moses had to do in a dire emergency was to call upon God and intervention would be forthcoming. The sober facts are much different. Once, in sheer frustration, Moses cried out to God,

> Why pick on me, to give me the burden of a
> people like this? Are they *my* children? Am I
> their father? ... I can't carry this nation by my-
> self! The load is far too heavy! If you are going
> to treat me like this, please kill me right now; it
> will be a kindness! Let me out of this impossible
> situation!                    (Num 11:11–12, 14–15)

This should be some gauge of how Moses was feeling about his endless failures. You may be sure that
many Christians—especially clergy—often feel this
way, too.

God, always looking at the heart, decided what was
best: Moses must go on loving these people whom he
probably wanted to up and leave on more than one
occasion. He was called upon to keep his head while
those around him freely lost theirs. Moses was not
given the prerogative of declaring himself mentally
bankrupt; he could not simply stay in his tent one
morning, when his responsibilities became too great
to bear, and say, 'Sorry, Chaps, I can't be bothered
any more: I'm at the end of my tether'. In the midst of
matters of life and death, he had to fall on his knees,
probably with his face to the ground, and beg God to
deliver ... even as the very people he was trying to
help—the Hebrews—openly condemned him.

Anne Townsend asks,

> How do I react when someone digs an emo-
> tional or verbal knife into me? Automatically, I
> want to fight back bitterly and to hurt as much—
> or more—as I have been hurt. Yet Jesus indi-
> cates that his children are to follow a different
> behaviour pattern —one that can only be theirs
> if he is allowed to change and control them.[5]

## It Only Hurts When I Grow

While few of us will ever be called upon to bear up under the staggering responsibility faced by Moses, what was happening to him is one of God's ways of helping his followers to grow. Often we want our lives and jobs to remain comfortable and easy, but with each added responsibility comes a new skill or ability, which often proves invaluable later on.

Moses was suffering. Moses was also growing. Just compare this leader to the one at the start of this chapter. No longer was he goaded on by his temper and ego to lash out in anger at any opposition. Like a thoroughbred horse, he needed to be broken in before being of any use to his owner.

Failure always brings conflict. Conflict may be used by God to help us achieve the humble and contrite spirit Jesus Christ himself demonstrated, or it may be the springboard which prompts us to curse God. In her book *Conflict*, author Joyce Huggett notes:

> Where conflict exists ... the Evil One, the father of lies, is ever-active. In order to become aware of his subversive role in this specific instance I ask myself, 'What is the *Evil One* whispering in my ear about this situation and the people involved?' I try to be objective; to bring the whispering alongside the truth.... I record Satan's subtle suggestions that often come in the form of condemnation or over-sensitivity or hurt feelings. In the parallel column I record the facts.
>
> This is not to say I deny my feelings. No. The next stage is to *express* the whole gamut of my feelings to God. Negative feelings need to be ventilated ... into the ear of an understanding God, he will sift them, keep what is worth keeping, and throw the rest away.[6]

Citing Paul's words in Romans 8:26, Huggett goes on

to suggest that speaking to God, even if it's only our 'sighs, groans and tears', is far better than silently wallowing in our own self-pity.

Moses cried out to God each time his people underscored his failures. As God spoke to Moses' heart, so Moses' confidence grew and grew in such adversity.

## Make Us A God!

Moses considered his greatest failure to have occurred while he was on Mount Sinai. In his absence, he appointed Aaron to be in charge of the assembly. Before long, the Hebrews had convinced Aaron to forge for them a golden calf, so they could worship it. This was because they feared Moses had died on the top of the mountain, and they sought another god to serve since their intermediary was no longer with them.

On the mountain, God told Moses what his people were up to and threatened to destroy them. Moses pleaded for the Israelites, and the Lord agreed to spare them. Moses then sped down the mountain, furious, and when he reached the plain below, he scolded Aaron bitterly. Deciding this was not enough, he challenged the priests and men from the tribe of Levi to rally round, and he made them kill the others for their part in the idol-worship ceremony. About 3,000 people died that day. This harsh judgement may be difficult for us to understand, but what Moses did the next day helps us to see that the charges were very serious indeed: 'Oh, these people have sinned a great sin, and have made themselves gods of gold. Yet now, if you will only forgive their sin—and if not, then blot me out of the book you have written [or kill me instead of them]' (Exod 32:31–32). Moses' willingness to sacrifice himself out of love for his sinful people was a remarkable foreshadowing of the love sacrifice Christ was to make for us, his equally sinful people.

## Jehovah Reaches The Places Others Cannot Touch

Frequently, I hear people excuse their failures by saying, 'I'm no saint.' They may have a distorted idea of true saints. Moses, the murderer and the failed politician, was a saint. So are all Christians, according to Paul.[7] As saints, we may lose our jobs, create strife, become jealous; in other words, we are prone to make mistakes and sin. Some sins will be small, and therefore easy to put out of our minds. However, other sins will be great, and we must not allow Satan to emasculate our faith with his incessant accusations when we do miss our self-imposed marks. He will be ever lurking, ready to criticise, denigrate and belittle us.

Most Bible commentaries agree that the incident at Mount Horeb, recorded in Exodus 17:6 and Numbers 20, represents Moses' greatest sin: combined egoism and a failure to trust God. At that time there was an acute lack of water and the people were, as usual, in a mutinous mood. Both Moses and Aaron sought God's help in the matter through strong prayer. Finally, God spoke, saying:

> 'Get Aaron's rod; then you and Aaron must summon the people. As they watch, speak to that rock over there and tell it to pour out its water!'...
> So Moses did as he was instructed. He took the rod from the place where it was kept before the Lord; then Moses and Aaron summoned the people to come and gather at the rock; and he said to them, 'Listen you rebels! Must we bring water from this rock?'
> Then Moses lifted the rod and struck the rock

twice, and water gushed out; and the people and
their cattle drank.                    (Num 20:8–11)

Sadly, Moses was quietly allowing his pride to
grow—and this led to his fall. Ostensibly, Moses did
as the Lord had commanded. However, a closer look
at the passage will reveal that he had in fact disobeyed
boldly. God wanted Moses to speak to the rock; instead he struck it because he was angry with the
people, whom he referred to in a derogatory way as
'rebels'. The taunt, 'Must we bring you water from
this rock?' denotes a tone of self-importance and a dis-
tinct lack of charity towards his fellows. Whether this
was a simple human error or a deliberate decision to
ignore God is not for us to say. What happened next,
however, sheds light on how God regarded this
action. The Lord said to Moses and Aaron: 'Because
you did not believe me and did not sanctify me in the
eyes of the people of Israel, you shall not bring them
into the land I have promised them' (Num 20:12).

After 40 years of hard struggle and all the severe
lessons he had learned, Moses, the Great Law Giver,
the man who spoke face to face with Jehovah, the deliverer of a whole nation, was not allowed to set foot in
the Promised Land because of this single act.

We may be inclined to think this was rather a harsh
punishment for something as benign as striking a rock
twice. After all, previously Moses murdered a man,
and God didn't punish him for that. Likewise, when
he first met God in the form of the burning bush,
Moses defied the Lord—but God remained fatherly,
albeit firm. Remember that God looks on the places
where the human eye cannot probe. Moses' previous
failings were not of the heart. The motive is what is
important to God. Moses became—for whatever
reason—inflated with his own self-importance at

Mount Horeb. This prompted him suddenly to look down on his brothers and sisters, perhaps fancying that he was better than they. God will not tolerate this attitude in his children. Paul teaches, 'Don't be selfish; don't live to make a good impression on others. Be humble, thinking of others as better than yourself' (Phil 2:3).

CS Lewis reminds us of this in *The Great Divorce*. When the day-trippers from hell see that people whom they had considered to be sinners are actually in heaven, they are dumbfounded. There are even murderers in heaven, while some bishops are in hell! This offensive revelation drives many of the most religious of the day-trippers back to the city of death, far below.[8]

With God it is not the sin as much as the intention that is of import. After all, Adam and Eve were dispossessed from Eden. Their crime? Eating a piece of fruit!

## A Father's Love For His Children

The true measure of Moses' character must be gauged at the end of his life. Moses composed a song of praise to God whom he had served for the last 40 years in the desert. Then, despite the ultimate failure—that of being denied the honour of being the one to lead his people into the Promised Land—he blessed each of the tribes in turn and then spoke to God. This now humble and fatherly man said to his God:

> O Jehovah, the God of the spirits of all mankind, [before I am taken away] please appoint a new leader for the people, a man who will lead them into battle and care for them, so that the people of the Lord will not be as sheep without a shepherd.                    (Num 27:15–17)

Are these the words of an unrepentant and failed political leader? Are they bitter, resentful words? Hardly. These are the loving words of a kindly father, concerned for the welfare of his children.

At the beginning of this chapter, we saw Moses the fugitive outlaw. Even if he had been captured and duly punished for his crime, it is unlikely that Moses' personality would have been improved to this extent. We may conclude that after God came into Moses' life, notwithstanding Horeb, his failures and disadvantages gradually were turned into blessings and advantages. In the eyes of the world, Moses may be considered a classic failure. Called by God to lead the children of Israel out of bondage into a Promised Land, Moses wandered aimlessly in the desert for 40 years. However, the crushing failure came at the end of Moses' days when the children of Israel at last came within sight of the Promised Land. At this crucial moment, God refused to allow Moses the honour of leading the Jews into their future homeland, preferring to give the honour to Joshua, who was surely no more than an infant at the beginning of the Exodus. If anyone had the right to be bitter, it was Moses. However, despite the outward appearance of failure, he continued to trust and obey.

Moses' testimony stands before us as an example that life is surely part joy and part conflict. As Anne Townsend wisely comments: 'We lose out if we cushion ourselves from life's painful experiences. We will lose the joy that God releases when pain and joy dance together in harmony.'[9]

## Notes

[1]Charles Colson, *Born Again* (Hodder & Stoughton Ltd: London, 1979).

[2]Rita Nightingale, *Freed For Life* (Tyndale House: Wheaton, IL, 1984).

[3]Noel Fellowes, *Killing Time* (Lion Publishing: Tring, 1986).

[4]James Fleming, *Personalities of the Old Testament* (Scribner's Sons, Ltd: London, 1951), p 13.

[5]Anne J Townsend, *Suffering Without Pretending* (Ark Publishing: London, 1980), p 76.

[6]Joyce Huggett, *Conflict: Friend or Foe?* (Kingsway Publications Ltd: Eastbourne, 1984), p 190.

[7]I am a Roman Catholic and well understand the practice of canonisation, but I use the biblical definition of *saint*, as found in both the testaments. That is, all who love the Lord and call him Saviour are saints. (See Pss 16:3; 30:4; 34:9; 37:28; 79:2; 116:15; Prov 2:8; Rom 12:13; 15:25; I Cor 1:2; 6:2; Eph 5:3; Col 1:26; I Tim 5:10; Philem 7; Rev 8:3; etc—Revised Standard Version.)

[8]CS Lewis, *The Great Divorce* (Fontana: London, 1971).

[9]Townsend, *op cit,* p 66.

# Chapter 7

# Man Of Passion

### Can You Make a Silk Purse Out of a Sow's Ear?

A silent figure steals along narrow back streets in a large Middle-Eastern city. He wears a heavy woollen cloak, hitched high on his neck to obscure his blunt profile. In his mind, every noise, every footstep, means he is surely being followed.

At the shrill yowl of a cat in heat, the man dodges down an alley, breaking into a canter until he reaches his destination. There he frantically pounds his fist on the door, then pauses. In the agonising seconds that pass, a whimper catches in his throat. Impatiently, he begins to pound again, bloodying his hairy knuckles on the rough splinters of the oak door.

At last a timid voice calls, 'What do you want?'

'Open up, will you! It's me!' he whispers through his teeth.

The door swings open and a gaunt man with a thick brown beard appears from inside. The red rims and dark circles under his eyes show he hasn't slept that night, and his lined face is ashen in the pale light of the dawn sky. 'Peter—where have you—?'

Grabbing James by his bony shoulders, Peter cuts off the question, 'This time I've really failed him, do you hear me?'

Taking Peter by the arm, the younger man whispers, 'I've failed him, too. Remember, I was in the Garden when they took him away.'

'No, for God's sake! It's worse than that. Just an hour ago, I denied knowing him three times—right when my testimony might have helped the Teacher. *Three times!*' Peter's voice suddenly thundered into the frosty air—'I denied him once for each year I knew him!'

James' eyes widened in terror, and he tugged Peter's arm. 'Get inside and shut up, you old fool. Do you want the centurions to know where we are?' With that the door slammed shut and all was quiet in the street.

When we fail to live up to our own expectations, it is very tempting to lash out in despair—just as Peter did on that Friday morning when Christ was rushed through his sham trail and sentenced to death on the Cross. Since admission to knowing Jesus would have been suicide, who could blame Peter for failing to tell the truth about his relationship with Christ?[1]

> Meanwhile, as Peter was sitting in the court-yard, a girl [who worked for the High Priest] came over and said to him,
> 'You were with Jesus, for both of you are from Galilee.'
> But Peter denied it loudly. 'I don't even know what you are talking about,' he angrily declared.
> Later, out by the gate, another girl noticed him and said to those standing around, 'This man was with Jesus—from Nazareth.'
> Again Peter denied it, this time with an oath. 'I don't even know the man,' he said.
> But after a while, the man who had been standing there came over to him and said, 'We know you are one of his disciples, for we can tell by your Galilean accent.'
> Peter began to curse and swear. 'I don't even know the man,' he said.
> And immediately the cock crowed. Then Peter remembered what Jesus had said, 'Before the

cock crows, you will deny me three times!' And
he went away, crying bitterly.  (Matt 26:69–75)

## Why Me, Lord?

This was not the first time Peter failed his Lord, and it
wasn't to be the last either. To be fair, the other 11
apostles had their share of failures. However, because
the Gospels are so full of Peter, and because Jesus
speaks most often to him, I have chosen to deal mainly
with Peter in this chapter.

On reflection, it is surprising how frequently Peter
fails as an apostle, considering that many scholars believe Jesus selected him among the Twelve to be the
leader of the band of men:

> Simon, Simon, Satan has asked to have you, to
> sift you like wheat, but I have pleaded in prayer
> for you that your faith should not completely
> fail. So when you have repented and turned to
> me again, strengthen and build up the faith of
> your brothers.                    (Luke 22:31–32)

After his death and resurrection, Jesus piques Peter
by repeatedly asking the question, 'Simon, son of
John, do you love me more than these others?'
Peter, grieved at the way Jesus repeatedly asks this
same question, replies: 'Lord, you know my heart;
you know who I [do].'

Jesus says, 'Then feed my little sheep' (John 21:15–
17). Christ was entrusting Peter and the Eleven to
carry on the work that he had begun. Although Peter
is honoured to be selected by the Lord to lead the
work, it is very significant to note the ignoble end that
awaits Peter if he chooses to follow Christ:

'When you were young, you were able to do as

you liked and go wherever you wanted to; but
when you are old, you will stretch out your
hands and others will direct you and take you
where you don't want to go.' Jesus said this to
let him know what kind of death he would die to
glorify God. Then Jesus told him, 'Follow me.'

(John 21:18–19)

Luke tells us that the first time Jesus came into
Peter's home, Peter's mother-in-law was seriously ill
and languishing on her bed. To everyone's utter delight, Jesus asked to see the woman. 'Standing by her
bedside he spoke to the fever, rebuking it, and immediately her temperature returned to normal and
she got up and prepared a meal for them' (Luke 4:39).
Although in the months that followed, Peter had seen
Christ heal other unwell people, this healing of his
own mother-in-law must have left a profound mark on
his mind—and on the minds of his family. It is easy to
understand, then, that when Peter subsequently gave
up his successful fishing business to follow Jesus, there
was no protest from his family, who were his partners
in the business.

Not long after, however, Jesus and his 12 followers
were out in a boat crossing a lake. As the men laboured
to navigate, Jesus decided to stretch out in the sun and
have a rest. While he was asleep, the wind came up,
and a storm descended upon the small sailing craft.
Although Luke does not mention any names, it is easy
to imagine Peter, the elected spokesman, shaking the
sleeping Christ, crying, 'Master, Master, we're sink-
ing!'

Christ turned his bearded face into the wind and
growled, 'Quieten down', with the firm authority of a
man secure in his ability to control the elements.
Then, turning to the Twelve—and no doubt eyeing
Peter—Jesus asked, 'Where is your faith?' Whatever

they replied outwardly, inwardly they were filled with fearful respect for Jesus, asking amongst themselves, 'Who is this man, that even the winds and waves obey him?' (Luke 8:22–25).

Once, Peter deftly put his foot in his mouth after a woman suffering from chronic haemorrhaging touched the hem of Christ's dusty robe, knowing Jesus would cure her.

Pivoting, Christ queried, 'Who touched me?'

Peter, who felt more comfortable alone on a beach at dawn with his nets, was agitated by the vast throng milling about. Tugging his beard with both hands and gazing at the crowd, Peter exploded, 'Master, so many are crowding against you....'

Jesus' reply once again put Peter in his place. 'No, it was someone who deliberately touched me, for I felt healing power go out from me.' Seconds later Peter learned that a woman had been cured by her faith, although she was deemed incurable by the finest physicians of that day (Luke 8:45–48).

After witnessing Christ's power time and again, one might think Peter would have thought better than to question the Master's cryptic statements. Certainly, Peter had more than an inkling of who Jesus was. After all, it was he who spoke for the Twelve when he answered Jesus' question, 'Who do you think I am?' Peter had answered correctly when he replied, 'The Messiah—the Christ of God' (Luke 9:20). Yet Peter continued to demonstrate his ignorance of Scripture and his propensity to make the mistakes which led to his well-documented failures.

When Jesus decided the time was right to explain about what was to become of him before he could establish himself as the rightful heir of the Father's kingdom, he referred to Isaiah, chapter 52, verse 13 and chapter 53, verses 1 to 12. Jesus taught the apostles that he '… would suffer, and that he would be rejected by the elders and the Chief Priests and the other Jewish leaders—and be killed, and that he would rise again three days afterwards' (Mark 8:31).

Not understanding the need for Jesus to die, Peter took Jesus aside later on and rebuked him. It would be easy to imagine this scene:

'Don't say such unthinkable things, Master,' said Peter puffing out his chest. 'After all, *we'll* protect you so you can go on doing your miracles. Nobody is going to kill you while we are here to guard you! Especially if *I'm* the leader of the group!'

'Jesus turned and looked at his disciples and then said to Peter very sternly, "Satan, get behind me! You are looking at this only from a human point of view and not from God's"' (Mark 8:33). Imagine Peter's chagrin—yet again he had spoken out of turn and even had to endure Christ's calling him *Satan*. I'm certain Peter wanted the earth to open up and swallow him. He may have even entertained serious thoughts of quietly slipping back to his nets rather than continue as a disciple.

Although no Scripture records this scene, it is easy to imagine Peter confronting Jesus tearfully, saying, 'You appointed the wrong man, Master. Why not make John the leader? You love him and he never seems to get it wrong. Or how about Philip? He's so *reliable*. I'm sure he'd better understand what you're on about when you talk about spiritual matters.' As always, the ever-lurking Satan would have been right at Peter's elbow, grinning to hear him fall for the old trick of comparing himself to others.

Still, Jesus knew exactly what qualities he wanted when he selected Peter as the first among the Twelve. JI Packer suggests that God uses the following criteria in evaluating men and women who say they want to serve him. Notice how each of the following may be said of Peter:

—'Those who know God have great energy for God': Peter was certainly ready to do anything and go anywhere for God. Jesus selected a man of action, not a dreamer, when he called the charismatic fisherman from his nets.

—'Those who know God have great thoughts of God': Peter and his brother, Andrew, were probably both disciples of John the Baptist during his ministry by the River Jordan, and while they had no formal rabbinic training, it is certain they made up for this with the keen eagerness of a disciple. (The word 'disciple' actually means 'pupil'.)

—'Those who know God show great boldness for God': After Jesus' ascension, Peter organised the first missionary movement. As he spoke he gave great inspiration to the apostles on Pentecost, and he was the first apostle to muster faith enough to perform a miracle in the name of Jesus—healing a cripple at the Beautiful Gate of the temple.

—'Those who know God have great contentment in God':[2] Later, after it became a state crime to confess Christ, Peter's letters reflect his willingness to endure harsh suffering at the hands of the Romans as a small price to pay for sharing in the brotherhood (and sisterhood) of Christ. (See The First Letter of Peter in the New Testament.)

Most significantly, notice the list of attributes does *not* include a fifth statement, reading: 'Those who know God have a perfect record of success while serving him.' If the latter were a prerequisite, then all the saints in the Old and New Testaments would have been eliminated systematically.

Through plentiful examples, I have aimed to prove that Christians are bound to err, sin and fail—sometimes miserably—as they attempt to serve God with the gifts and talents they possess. However, the goal to keep in view is that, even though we often lose skirmishes and small battles, we never fail in the eternal sense. The war has already been won by Jesus. Those instances that arise and cause misadventure for Christians can be likened to the small battles that raged across Europe in April 1945. Victory in Europe had been declared in favour of the Allies. Even as Hitler planned his suicide in his impregnable *Führerbunker*, many squadrons of Nazis fought on in vain. Their bullets and bayonets were lethal, yes, but they were acting on borrowed time. Before long, the word was widespread that Hitler and the cause of the oppressors no longer existed.

It is the same with the Christian experience. Christians have the assurance of victory, even though conflict often faces them in the meantime. Paul writes of a hope that lies in the future:

> O death, where then your victory? Where then your sting? For sin—the sting that causes death—will all be gone; and the law, which reveals our sins, will no longer be our judge. How we will thank God for all this! It is he who makes us victorious through Jesus Christ our Lord!
>
> (I Cor 15:55–57)

## Let Go And Let God

Christ's Sermon on the Mount makes it clear that being a Christian requires great humility. The well-known minister of Westminster Chapel Martyn

Lloyd-Jones, comments on Matthew 5:1–12: 'these Beatitudes as they proceed become increasingly difficult … [they are] more searching, more difficult, more humbling and even more humiliating.'[3]

Staying with the example of Peter, the best-known incident where he failed to understand this concept of humility was the time he saw Christ walking towards their boat across rough seas—as recorded in Matthew chapter 14, verses 22 to 33.

Perhaps Peter wanted desperately to show Jesus that he did have faith. Peter bade Christ to call him out on to the water. When Jesus complied, Peter clambered over the side of the boat and began walking towards Jesus. Certainly it was not through Peter's own herculean effort that he walked on the water. That he could have even stood on the sea and not sunk is a wonderful illustration of the words found in Mark chapter 10, verse 27: 'But with God everything is possible.' Peter managed to let go of his own ego for one bright moment and allow Jesus to call him forth.

Of course, there was a third person out on the sea at that time, though the Scriptures do not point him out. It was Satan. If we were to have a picture of the unseen realm at that moment in history, we would see grandstands of spiritual creatures looking on to see what would happen.[4]

In the film *Time Bandits*, the Monty Python crew are engaged in the struggle between good and evil in the universe. While I hardly can commend John Cleese and company for their keen theological insights, the way they depicted Satan's influence over his victims was particularly good. The Devil's second-person suggestions entered the human mind as first-person thoughts. Here is how Satan may have prompted Peter to stop trusting Jesus and start trusting himself.

**Satan:** Peter, my good man, you're a fisherman and well acquainted with the laws of nature. Don't you know that it is impossible for you to be walking on water?

**Peter:** Help! My feet are getting wet! I must be crazy for trying to walk on water!

**Satan:** Well, you're out there now and everyone is looking at you. Whatever happens, Old Boy, you *must* save face. Do hurry up before you begin to sink.

**Peter:** Good grief, what'll the lads think of me if I muck this up? Maybe I should start to run.

**Satan:** Jesus will *never* let you forget it if you blow it *again*. Have faith in *yourself* and you can do it!

**Peter:** I can do it. I *know* I can do it! I—*Aaahhii!*

But it was too late. He was terrified and began to sink. 'Save me, Lord!' he shouted. And once again, Jesus had to criticise Peter for setting out in faith, but then giving in to the human temptation of trying to please God on his own.

The Swiss psychiatrist Paul Tournier writes in *The Adventure of Living* that we court failure when we try too hard. 'A thing that strikes one in the daily practice of psychology is that the people who fail are those who try hardest to succeed … they try so hard and are so anxious that they fail.'[5] Perhaps over-anxiousness to succeed was Peter's problem. When he lost faith in Jesus' strength, he immediately began to rely on his own. The result was inundating! Peter's anxiety to succeed created a spirit-killing fear: fear takes away joy and confidence and turns the mind inward on self, rather than outward on God. Tournier maintains that this soon becomes a vicious circle. Of course, the longer the circle continues, the less prepared we are to accept our failures as anything short of punishment from God or evidence of our own inadequacy—and the harder it becomes to break the circle.

Fortunately, Peter called out to Jesus whom he knew and loved. Indeed, it was his love for Jesus that saved him in the end. 'Amid all Peter's stumbles and falls, this always brought him right again and set him on his feet again—his absolutely enthusiastic love and adoration for his master.'[6]

Notwithstanding Peter's love for Jesus, it still did not prevent him from failing. At the opening of this chapter, we saw Peter at what was perhaps the lowest ebb in his life—the day he denied Christ three times. Speaking from a comfortable distance of nearly 2,000 years, and with the benefit of hindsight, it is tempting to imagine that if I had spent 3 years in the intimate company of the Messiah; if he had cured my mother-in-law of a deathly illness; if I had been there to see Jesus calm the waters and raise the dead back to life— then *surely* on that first Good Friday morning, I would have been bold enough to say to the accusing crowds: 'Yes, you're right. I do know him. And I also know that he is being framed by his enemies!' And in my mind's eye, I see myself trooping boldly into the Jewish Supreme Court, shouting for effect, 'As each of you know, I have been with Jesus constantly for three years; therefore, my testimony is better than anything you pack of vipers could patch together. I say he *is* the Messiah!'

Of course this bit of bravado is nothing more than an optimistic exercise of my imagination. The truth is, if the myriad of untoward incidents in my life—times when I have made mistakes, chosen not to get involved, or have stood by in frozen indecision whilst someone else suffered—is any criterion to go on, then it is very likely that *I*, too, would have denied knowing

Christ. Too often we are over-confident of our devotion to Christ—just as Peter was. We must always be humble—and prepared to admit our weaknesses.

I am aware that some may argue Peter's failures happened prior to Pentecost. As the Holy Spirit was not yet upon Peter or the apostles, the argument goes, they were incapable of dealing with the problems Spirit-filled Christians take in their stride. This is a fair argument. The difference between the apostles before and after the descending of the Holy Spirit is like the difference between the hills of the North Downs and the mountain peaks of the Himalayas. Neither hills nor mountains are flat, but certainly Everest is far more spectacular in dimension than Box Hill in the South-East of England! The Holy Spirit gives us an extra dimension.

The fearless deaths of Peter, James and others contrast sharply with the earlier pictures of them when they huddled like fugitives from the law in rooms with bolted doors and shuttered windows. Suddenly, it was as though the doors were unbolted and they became instruments in the making of thousands of converts. This never could have happened without the benefit of the Holy Spirit. However, the Holy Spirit is *not* an insurance against failure. To suggest as much would be a hollow promise indeed.

### 'For Now We See In A Mirror Darkly'

Paul, speaking well after Pentecost, makes it clear:

> When I was a child, I spoke and thought and reasoned as a child does. But when I became a man, my thoughts grew far beyond those of my childhood, and now I have put away the childish things. In the same way, we can see and understand only a little about God now, as if we were

> peering at his reflection in a poor mirror; but
> some day we are going to see him in his com-
> pleteness, face to face. Now all that I know is
> hazy and blurred, but then I will see everything
> clearly, just as clearly as God sees into my heart
> right now.                    (I Cor 13:11–12)

In Acts 10, Peter has a vision from the Lord in which
he is ordered to include non-kosher food in his diet.
Here is an example of how even the Spirit-filled
apostle continues to misconstrue God's will. Although Peter has already been through this all-too-
familiar scenario many times in the past, and though
he now has the help of the Holy Spirit, his impetuous
reply is, 'Never, Lord ... I have never in all my life
eaten such creatures, for they are forbidden by our
Jewish laws' (Acts 10:14).

Peter presumes to tell *God* what the Law requires
of good Jews! God, using a supernatural medium—a
vision—has to speak strongly to get through Peter's
thick hide: 'Don't contradict God! If he says something is kosher, then it is' (Acts 10:15).

Peter's stubbornness is hard to believe: the vision
had to be repeated *three times* before the apostle
would accept that God was ordering him to eat pork,
shellfish and certain 'unclean' birds. What is Peter's
problem?

The crux of this problem is twofold. Peter is loaded
down with cultural bias, so firmly ingrained in his out-
look that it is almost part of his personality; he is also
displaying pride by presuming to know God's will
better than God himself. We shouldn't be too harsh in
judging Peter's failings, though. Ever since the Fall,
man has been making dogmatic assertions regarding
God's behaviour. The writer of Proverbs 20:24
advises, 'Since the Lord is directing our steps, why try

to understand everything that happens along the way?' We cannot presume to know *absolutely* God's will.

Peter's notion that he knew more about God's will than God could have been the first step towards another of his classic failures. This time, however, Peter is saved by his heartfelt desire to do God's will, opaque as it may have seemed. Although human beings cannot put God in a neat little pigeon hole, we may take comfort in what the psalmist says, 'The steps of good men are directed by the Lord. He delights in each step they take. If they fall, it isn't fatal, for the Lord holds them in his hand' (Ps 37:23–24).

Shortly after this, Peter is sent for by the Roman centurion, Cornelius—a hated Gentile—who begs Peter to preach the Word so he can become a follower of Jesus Christ. Normally Peter would not have entered the home of a Gentile. Although Peter's actions were considered unorthodox, he was in fact doing God's will.

In the next chapter of Acts, we read of Peter's problems when he arrived back in Jerusalem. The Jewish believers said angrily, 'You fellowshipped with Gentiles and even ate with them' (Acts 11:3).

Suddenly, Peter finds himself defending evangelism to the Gentiles, despite what the Law taught about the need to be wholly separate. Until this time, Christianity had been exclusively Jewish. While the church in Jerusalem was Spirit-filled, it was also ignorant of God's fuller plan of salvation. It was Peter who acted as God's spokesman in order to put things right in the neophyte church.

## The Right Stuff

Why did Jesus select Peter? It is true that 'John was in-

tuitive, meditative, mystical. Philip was phlegmatic,
... [but] Peter was sanguine and enthusiastic and extreme both for good and for evil, beyond them all.'[7]
When Christ selected Peter to fill the leadership role
for the band of 12, he was not looking on the outside
where men look when they make value judgements.
He peered into the heart of Peter which was one given
naturally to contrition:

> One day as he [Jesus] was preaching on the
> shore of Lake Gennesaret, great crowds pres-
> sed in on him to listen to the Word of God. He
> noticed two empty boats standing at the water's
> edge while the fishermen washed their nets.
> Stepping into one of the boats, Jesus asked
> Simon [Peter], its owner, to push out a little into
> the water, so that he could sit in the boat and
> speak to the crowds from there.
>
> When he had finished speaking, he said to
> Simon, 'Now go out where it is deeper and let
> down your nets and you will catch a lot of fish!'
>
> 'Sir,' Simon replied, 'we worked hard all last
> night and didn't catch a thing. But if you say so,
> we'll try again.'
>
> And this time their nets were so full that they
> began to tear! A shout for help brought their
> partners in the other boat and soon both boats
> were filled with fish and on the verge of sinking.
>
> When Simon Peter realised what had hap-
> pened, he fell to his knees before Jesus and said,
> 'Oh, sir, please leave us—I'm too much of a sin-
> ner for you to have around.'          (Luke 5:1–8)

Christ, sensing the contrite heart of this pugnacious
fisherman, replied with an enigmatic twinkle, 'Don't
be afraid! From now on you'll be fishing for the souls
of men!' (Luke 5:10).
This reply to Peter's candid admission embodies the

patience Jesus shows towards all who fall short of their ideals. For Christ did not respond by saying, 'Oh, yes, well, you'll have to stop sinning first, of course, if you're to come and follow me.' Jesus calls us *as we are*, and changes come in various degrees and at different stages in our lives. As Charles Wesley wrote, 'He wants nothing of godliness, but the power; nothing of religion, but the spirit; nothing of Christianity, but the truth and life.'[18]

Put another way, Peter's tendency to be hot or cold, depending on the circumstances, is apparently what God looks for in each of us. God would prefer a whole-hearted error to a half-hearted attempt at doing what is right. The proof is found in Revelation 3:15–16. 'I know you well—you are neither hot nor cold; I wish you were one or the other! But since you are merely lukewarm, I will spit you out of my mouth!' Much may be said about Peter, but he can *never* be described as lukewarm.

One might conclude that, contrary to the old English proverb, Christ *is* in the business of making silk purses out of sows' ears. In any case, it is important to keep in mind the fact that Peter, more than the other 11 apostles, possessed what Tom Wolf, in his book by the same title, has called 'The Right Stuff'. The evidence lies in Peter's life and the service he rendered to his Lord until the apostle's death. More than any of the other apostles, including Judas Iscariot, Peter made blunders that could have ruined his chances of serving God. After each failure, he picked up the pieces, learned from his errors, and tells all who fail while serving Christ,

In this you rejoice, though now for a little while you may have to suffer various trials, so that the genuineness of your faith, more precious than

gold which though perishable is tested by fire,
may redound to praise and glory and honour at
the revelation of Jesus Christ.

(I Peter 1:6–7 [RSV])


## Notes

[1]Ostensibly, Peter denied knowing Christ three times
owing to fear. However, some Bible commentaries
claim that Peter may have lied about being a follower
of Christ in order not to be called before the court to
testify to Jesus' claim of being the Messiah, which
would have been deemed as evidence of Christ's blas-
phemy.
[2]JI Packer, *Knowing God* (Hodder & Stoughton Ltd:
London, 1975), pp 24–28.
[3]Frank Cumbers (ed), *The First Book of Daily Readings from the Works of Martyn Lloyd-Jones* (Epworth
Press: London, 1970), p 197.
[4]I Peter 1:12 makes it clear that the events going on in
the human realm are so significant that even angels
look on with interest. Francis Schaeffer once commented that we would be terrified at the awesome
prospect we would encounter if we could but see the
battle raging in the spiritual realm. Of Satanic influence on mortals, author and evangelist Nicky Cruz
writes,

> Whenever I preach, I am conscious of two
> others on the platform beside me. I know Jesus
> is there with me. I know ... that Satan is there
> too ... I know that the struggle between Satan
> and Jesus is always taking place, and will never
> end until this age itself ends.
> (Nicky Cruz, *Satan On the Loose* [Oliphants:
> London, 1973], p 80)

[5]Paul Tournier, *The Adventure of Living* (SCM Press Ltd: London, 1976), p 108.
[6]Alexander Whyte, *Bible Characters—The New Testament*, vol 2 (Marshall, Morgan & Scott Publications Ltd: London, 1972), p 39.
[7]*ibid.*
[8]John Telford (ed), *Sayings and Portraits of Charles Wesley* (Epworth Press: London, 1927), p 20.

# Chapter 8

# 'Not My Will, But Thine'

### Show Me!

Many long for God to come to earth and demonstrate his power today, as he did in ancient times—then they would surely know what they believed and why. This is hardly symptomatic of modern scepticism. At Jesus' trial, King Herod hoped to see a miracle, for he too had heard of this Jewish rabbi who could raise the dead. Like an eager little boy, Herod 'asked Jesus question after question, but there was no reply' (Luke 23:8–9). The many people assembled for the extravaganza, which was Christ's execution on the cross, also wanted to see with their own eyes.

> 'Ha! Look at you now!' they yelled at him. 'Sure, you can destroy the temple and rebuild it in three days!' If you're so wonderful, save yourself and come down from the cross…. You "King of Israel"! Come on down from the cross and we'll believe you!' (Mark 15:29–30, 32)

Of course, no sign was given under such circumstances. Why? God certainly wants people to know of his power, but he will not be manipulated. Being a human being, Jesus understood the problem of our natural agnosticism: 'How privileged you are to see what you have seen,' he once said to his disciples who enjoyed the benefit of seeing his power in action many times. 'Many a prophet and king of old has longed for these days, to see and hear what you have seen and heard!' (Luke 10:23–24).

Many Christians living since the time of the apostles have been locked into a comparatively dreary, unglamorous, materialistic life with very little dramatic evidence to validate their faith in Christ. Certainly we must appear to be fools in the eyes of an unbelieving world when we turn the other cheek, tithe our income, and worship an unseen Jesus in dance, word and song. Gone are the burning bushes, voices from the clouds and pillars of fire to lead us to victory. Gone, too, are afternoons by the sea with the Son of God as he cures the blind and then turns to explain to us our glorious destiny.

Though God's reality may not be proved in the laboratory or the court room, proof of his existence may still be found everywhere today. All around the world there is evidence of God's presence—Christian bookshops are filled with books, records and tapes that describe and proclaim God's goodness. Since this is so, why doesn't everyone claim to know God? Perhaps it is because God chooses to reveal himself in a singularly unpopular way: often in human weakness. Most people are looking in the skies for awesome signs and wonders, and so miss the most tangible proof of God's existence close-by.

In her book *Tramp for the Lord*, Corrie ten Boom suggests that in human frailty, weakness, and even in what appears to be hopeless failure, God is there working out his will using people no one would ever suspect of being his agents: the humble, the poor, the dejected and the infirm.

Corrie tells of an old woman in Russia who lived with her devoted husband. Her body was horribly bent and twisted, and she had lost all bodily control except for one finger. Anyone who saw this woman, including Corrie ten Boom, would conclude that, in terms of quality of life, she was not much better than a vegetable. But in God's eyes she was a valued messenger of the gospel behind the Iron Curtain.

Each day, and well into the night, this amazing woman sat propped up with pillows in front of a manual typewriter. There she pecked feebly at the clumsy, old machine, translating 'Christian books into Russian, Latvian, and the language of her people. Always using just that one finger—peck ... peck ... peck —she typed out the pages. Portions of the Bible, the books of Billy Graham, Watchman Nee.'[1]

According to her husband, not only did this woman type manuscripts, she also prayed ceaselessly as she worked.[2]

Corrie could hardly look at this pitiful creature, a tangle of severely curled limbs beneath her body. Corrie wondered why the Lord did not heal his faithful servant. Guessing Corrie's thoughts, the old woman's husband pointed out that God had a purpose for allowing his wife to remain painfully crippled: her failed health is God's secret weapon against the dark powers of the Soviet police. He said,

> Every other Christian in the city is watched by
> the secret police. But because she has been sick
> so long, no one ever looks in on her. They leave
> us alone and she is the only person in the city
> who can type quietly, undetected by the police.[3]

The world looks in vain for great signs of power and majesty. But Jesus, the master of irony, says to his disciples, '[Only] You are permitted to know some truths about the kingdom of God that are hidden to those outside the kingdom: "Though they see and hear, they will not understand or turn to God, or be forgiven for their sins"' (Mark 4:11–12).

Matthew puts it this way:

> His disciples came and asked him, 'Why do you
> always use these hard-to-understand illustra-
> tions?'
> Then he explained to them that only they
> were permitted to understand about the king-
> dom of heaven, and others were not....
> 'This fulfils the prophecy of Isaiah:
> "They hear, but don't understand;
> They look, but don't see!
> For their hearts are fat and heavy,
> and their ears are dull, and they
> have closed their eyes in sleep,
> so they won't see and hear and
> understand and turn to God again,
> and let me heal them".'
>
> (Matt 13:10–11, 14–16)

When I was an undergraduate, I had a favourite
English literature professor whom I'll call Dr Morgan.
One day we were discussing TS Eliot's Christianity,
and my professor referred to this same passage in
Matthew chapter 13. According to Dr Morgan, this
teaching was evidence that Christianity is hopelessly
élitist—it is like some sort of club which accepts only
'initiated' people.

I had only recently been converted to Christianity
out of profound agnosticism, and so remained quiet,
not knowing enough about Christianity to enter into
an argument. Other than the fact that I knew I had
given my life to Christ, my knowledge of Christian
doctrine could at that time have been summed up on
one 3″ by 5″ note card. Yet inwardly I disagreed
whole-heartedly with Dr Morgan.

For one thing, I certainly did not consider myself
*élite*. Nor had I been *initiated*. As Groucho Marx once

said, 'I certainly wouldn't join a club that was willing to admit someone like *me* as a member.' And that's how I felt about the Church.

My first step towards embracing Christianity occurred one night as I was coming home from a party with my friends, including Dominic DeCusatis—whose death I mentioned in the dedication of this book. We happened to hear a man preaching the gospel on a street corner. This was too much fun to pass up, so my friends and I stood there and began to fire endless questions at this poor man, hardly allowing him to reply before we challenged him again. When we got tired of that sport, we simply walked away—laughing off his invitation to accept Christ as our saviour.

I'm sure this man went home that night heavy-hearted, telling his wife that he felt an utter fool and a failure. Yet, oddly enough, what I had heard made sense. Whether it was my early Catholic training, or whether it was the work of the Holy Spirit, I don't know. However, even as an agnostic, I was aware of sin in my own life, though I doubt I would have used so theological a word as 'sin'—I might have used the word guilt instead. Anyway, as a result of hearing that night that God had sent Jesus to die on the Cross in my place, to take on the guilt and punishment I deserved for my sins, I began to make my own investigations into the claims of the Bible.

Ignoring the Old Testament, I began with the Gospel of John. I was amazed at what God had to say: anyone may repent and find everlasting life—no matter how good or how bad they are. It really is that simple. (Perhaps my saying this will cause some to think that my knowledge of Christian doctrine has not increased much over the last 15 years!) Nevertheless, the World Council of Churches' theological secretary, Alan PF Sell, makes the same point, 'If we do not have to be good enough to merit salvation, we certainly do not have to be good enough to pray for it.'⁴

I think that for years, I had been expecting some sign or evidence to be presented to me before I would take God seriously. 'Show me' was my motto. The problem is we can neither see nor understand God. That's why Jesus mostly ignores demands for miracles and irrefutable proof as a means of converting the unbelieving. After all, the apostles watched Jesus closely for three years. They saw his wonderful miracles. Yet each promptly forgot them when Christ was arrested —despite what they had seen with their own eyes! Would we be any different?

The words spoken to Thomas, the doubter, recorded by the apostle John, suggest that even if God were to return to earth tomorrow to demonstrate his power over the universe, seeing would *still* not produce belief. Moreover, in some inexplicable way, it is actually better to believe without seeing. Note the irony in Jesus' words: 'Then Jesus told [Thomas], ... "You believe because you have seen me. But blessed are those who haven't seen me [and my miracles] and believe anyway"' (John 20:29).

Paul teaches that salvation comes from trusting God:

> For it is by believing in his heart that man becomes right with God; and with his mouth, he tells others of his faith, confirming his salvation. For the Scriptures tell us that no one who believes in Christ will be disappointed.... But not everyone who hears the Good News has welcomed it, for Isaiah the prophet said, 'Lord, who has believed me when I told them?' Yet faith comes from listening to this Good News— the Good News about Christ.
>
> (Rom 10:10–11, 16–17)

Nowhere in Scripture does it suggest that faith comes only by seeing.

As for my professor's charge that Christianity is an exclusive clique: the Christian experience is anything but élitist. On the contrary. A year after meeting that street evangelist, I had become a Christian while at university. During the summer break, I returned home and met my friend Dominic DeCusatis on the street and found that he, too, had become a believer over the past year—and the two of us had been the evangelist's loudest critics that night.

It is a blessing that there is such rich variety among the people who *do* come to know God—Greek Orthodox communicants share their church building with Russian Orthodox believers in Oxford; convicted prisoners take bread and grape juice from an ex-convict named Charles Colson in a sweltering prison in Dade County, Florida; Red Indians listen to Moral Majority's Jerry Falwell speak on radio in Montana; Chinese peasants attend a Bible study in a recently reopened Roman Catholic church in Baotou; Hungarian Pentecostals meet in a tiny flat in Miskolc; Nigerians beat out a rhythm on a drum in their church service at Ibadan; middle-class Lutherans shiver in an ancient cathedral in Munich; groups of born-again believers mass for a revival service in Cartagena, Colombia; a group of Episcopalian Arabs meet in Amman, Jordan, for a fellowship supper consisting of couscous and figs; the Queen Mother of Great Britain sends a copy of CS Lewis' *Mere Christianity* to one of her footmen when she hears he recently became a Christian at a Billy Graham crusade—these snapshots are evidence that Christ is determined to save as many as are willing to come to him. No door is too strong to keep the Spirit of God away from those who sincerely seek him. Christianity a clique? Hardly.

### 'Then Shall Your Light Break Forth Like The Dawn, And Your Healing Shall Spring Up Speedily'
#### (Isa 58:8 [RSV])

I heard the following story told by a Welsh pastor in the United States. Years ago when he was a lad growing up in a village near Rhondda, there was an accident in a mine. Some timbers had given way and a whole section of an underground passage had collapsed, sealing off nine men from the main shaft. A tenth man had escaped being sealed off with the others because he was nearest the entrance of the collapsed passageway. Nonetheless, he was pinned from the waist down beneath a pile of shattered timbers and rubble.

Immediately a rescue team was on its way with lanterns, picks and shovels. When they came across this man, he adamantly waved them on, shouting, 'No, no. Leave me. I'll be all right. The lads'll suffocate under that pile unless you start digging now! You just leave me a lamp and I'll sort myself out.'

Seeing that the man was in no pain, they gave him a lamp and moved on, leaving him to free himself while they began the long task of freeing the nine trapped miners.

Using an oak post as a lever and a rock as a fulcrum, the miner eased several large stones and some splintered timbers off his legs. When at last he removed most of the debris, he picked up the lantern and had a look at his lower half. Suddenly his eyes widened and he began to shriek pitifully for the others to come back to help him: his right leg had been severed above the knee by a sharp piece of metal and he knew only immediate medical attention would prevent his bleeding to death.

When it comes to God's offer of salvation, many people are like this self-sufficient miner. We feel that

God's offer is not an urgent priority, that we're fine, although others may need God's help. 'Matters of consequence' such as the day to day routine of working, paying bills, playing and sleeping, anaesthetise our spiritual nerve endings, crowding out the light, and making us feel comfortable, when in actual fact—spiritually—we are in great jeopardy. The miner was blissfully ignorant of his life's blood draining out of his body into the gritty soil of the mine shaft until he held up his light and saw for himself how near to death he was.

> If we are living in the light of God's presence, just as Christ does, then we have wonderful fellowship and joy with each other, and the blood of Jesus his son cleanses us from every sin. [But] if we say we have no sin, we are only fooling ourselves, and refusing to accept the truth.
>
> (I John 1:7–8)

Naturally, when the miner saw his true condition under the clear light of his lantern, he didn't think twice about calling out for help. As a result, his story had a happy ending—although the man lost his leg, he saved his life.

## Failure Is Like A Light

Failure sometimes can be the light which shows people their true condition. When everything is going smoothly, we tend to think that we do not need God's help, thank you. It is easy enough to fall prey to this type of thinking, too. But when the astringency of failure jolts us back into true perspective, we then see clearly how weak and helpless we are. Failure proves we are not independent. This, then, may be another reason why God allows Christians to fail.

Dorothy L Sayers, successful detective novelist and respected scholar, suffered a broken love affair which was followed by a profound social failure. Later on, she was married to a man who was hard to love. Put simply, despite her fame as a writer, Sayers knew what it was to be a failure.

As did so many of her generation, Sayers grew up accepting the orthodoxy of the Church of England. But by the time she had left Oxford University, she probably suspected that faith was a comfortable habit. On one hand, she was inured to church-going and regular worship, but on the other, she was acutely aware that there was no kick to much of what passed as Christianity: it seemed bloodless, mundane and cold. Out of sheer convention, she continued to attend church services, although it is arguable that Sayers maintained a spark which kept alive the embers of a burning faith ignited during her childhood.

When Sayers was in her thirties, she was well known for her Lord Peter Wimsey stories. Many people think that being a published author brings with it a sense of having *made it*. The truth is, Sayers had made many costly sacrifices and even flew in the face of convention to achieve distinction as a writer. (Male writers dominated the detective markets then—although today when we think of this genre, the first names which spring to mind are Dorothy L Sayers, Margery Allingham, Ngaio Marsh, Josephine Tey and Agatha Christie—all women.)

Years before, when Dorothy L Sayers had been in France, she had fallen in love with an artistically refined but emotionally crude man, who was incapable of returning Sayers' intense affection. Over the years, this lover repeatedly refused to answer Dorothy's plaintive overtures of love. While publishing did bring in money to make ends meet for Sayers, she was lonely and unfulfilled romantically. To compensate, she sought amorous fulfilment amongst the Bohemian set of Soho and Bloomsbury, but this, too, proved unsatisfactory.

Soon the novelist dropped all artistic airs as well as her Christian prudence. She sought instead fun and full sexual fulfilment with a plain, uneducated man who enjoyed motoring, drinking, smoking and dancing. Dorothy's Bloomsbury friends wondered what she saw in this man: they could hardly imagine what the couple talked about—she, a brilliant Oxford graduate and he, an uncouth mechanic. But he gave her a good time—as well as a son. Of course, Sayers wanted to marry her new lover, but she had managed once again to land herself with a cold and hardhearted man. He took not the slightest interest in Sayers, nor his child—who was eventually sent to live in Oxford with a relative. Sayers succumbed to the failure she had hoped to escape: she was a woman alone, only now she had to shoulder the added responsibility of a fatherless child.

No longer holding out for romance or a proper church wedding, Sayers met and married a journalist, some years her senior and also a divorcee. They were not in love in the conventional sense of the word.

Sayers is far too complex a character to be treated in so cursory a manner as I am doing here, but suffice it to say it was because her life had plumbed the depths that she was able to discover the reality of the Christian God. The Holy Spirit proved, even to the novelist's highly logical mind, that God was God. Soon after, Dorothy L Sayers was making a name for herself as a forthright lay theologian and apologist, in addition to writing popular drama and fiction.

James Brabazon, Sayers' biographer, claims that her evangelical zeal was not so much a result of her assurance of her own salvation, but more as a result of her understanding of the sordidness of sin.[5] In any case, this highly unconventional woman was busy making a case for the Christian religion—a reluctant evangelist if ever there was one.

In the 1940s she was asked by JW Welch, then Director of Religious Broadcasting for the BBC, to write a series of plays for release on the airwaves in monthly intervals over the period of December 1941 to October 1942. Sayers called the series *The Man Born To Be King*. Writing the foreword to the book of the same name in 1945, Welch commends Sayers' work as nothing short of brilliant—not only in terms of her craftsmanship as playwright, but in her ability to shed new light on an old subject: the life of Jesus Christ.

> For many, Christ is a man ... who is not relevant today ... he belongs to the teaching of a remote childhood or bad stained glass and effeminate pictures. Is it, or is it not true, that through Miss Sayers' use of realism, modern speech and the introduction of the character of our Lord, the person and life and teaching of Christ take on a new meaning and relevance? The answer which, I believe, the two million people who heard these plays would unhesitatingly give is, 'Yes'. As one secretary who had to type out the early plays said, 'But I never believed Christ *really lived!*'[6]

If Sayers had not stood naked in the harsh light of failure, humiliation, sexual frustration and—earlier in her career—the threat of financial hard times, Christianity might have remained for her no more than a watered-down, man-made religion. Had she not known Christ to be reliable no doubt Dorothy

Sayers would have turned her keen intellect and acid pen against the Church in the manner of Bernard Shaw or Bertrand Russell. She would not have been capable of writing this highly-charged cycle of plays, which at first was met with howls of harsh criticism, only to be later acclaimed by hundreds of thousands of BBC listeners and theologians all around the English-speaking world. It is important to note that God would not have brought about a change in Sayers to make *her* more effective, but rather to bring more glory to himself.

When failure embitters us, there is one thing we may be sure of. Because Christ emptied himself of his self-sufficiency as the Lord of the universe to become a man, he can identify with human failure; so when the foundations of our lives are about to crack, Jesus stands there with open arms, waiting for us to call on him. It is up to us to invite God into our lives. There is no élitism.

## The Last Half-hour

A few years ago, I had breakfast in a Glasgow café with a friend whom I'll call Charlie. Although he had agreed to come along to one or two services with me, he is not what I would describe as a church-goer, and he makes no apology for it. As we lingered over cups of strong, hot tea, Charlie leaned forward and gave me a level stare, saying, 'You're always going on about the suffering of Christ and all that. But it seems to me that if I knew *I* was the Messiah, I'd be willing to suffer and die on a cross too—especially if I knew that I'd only be dead for a few days, then I'd come back in a shining, new body.' He raised the steaming cup to his lips and took a sip, then continued, 'Those last few hours of humiliation, failure and suffering would be a small price to pay for the huge reward of being the king of the whole universe. Do you get what I mean?'

Although I did get his point, I don't agree with Charlie. Even if the Gospel accounts were written with the skill of a master novelist, it is still unlikely they could ever convey the depth of the anguish Christ suffered, not only at the end of his life, but also during the cryptic hidden years that John refers to at the end of his Gospel. He says there were far too many episodes in the life of Jesus for any one book to contain (John 21:25). We may be sure there were other unrecorded struggles which Christ had to endure in order to prepare for his life's sole purpose. Charlie's simplistic comments reflect every human being's ignorance regarding Christ's spiritual and physical suffering which was equal to, if not greater than, even the greatest human suffering we could name.

## What Do You Say To Someone Who Has Failed?

Don't be afraid of failure. Keep going on in spite of it. Worship God until victory comes. The hardest part of faith is the last half hour. Keep going, and you will yet face your finest hour. In the epilogue of this book, I'll have more to say about this difficult question.

### Bob and Marge's Story

Although I have changed their names, Bob and Marge Taylor are a young couple whom my wife and I met in Oxford.

Bob had brought his family to England from the United States in order to work on a DPhil in theology. As the years passed, Bob set his heart on becoming a university lecturer. He felt ill-suited to preaching and pastoral work. My wife and I knew that the Taylors had sacrificed much—financially and otherwise—in order for Bob to study at Oxford, but we had no doubts when they left for the United States that Bob would be sure to find work. Last Christmas we received this letter from Marge.

Dear Michael and Judith,
     After an autumn snowfall yesterday, the brilliance of the sun is warming the earth today and Bob has taken all four boys outdoors for a romp in the wet leaves. (I'm sure they'll all find lots of mud as well!) I am determined to finish this letter to you which I have been yearning to write for so long ... it seems a world of events have taken place since [last Christmas] ... and it seems much, much longer than a short 10 months ago.
     In January we were still residing in Oxford, during which time Bob was fervently rewriting and pushing so hard to finish his DPhil. That was such an extremely intense and stressful time with proof-reading, typing, final revision.... The latter part of March, he officially submitted his thesis to the Faculty of Theology, then waited for a date for his oral examination. That took place in April, with a victorious outcome for which we were much relieved and very over-whelmed—it seemed almost too good to be true. The final touch was for Bob to attend a degree ceremony in May.
     Then came the difficult task of packing up to return to the States; but the *most* difficult experience was saying 'goodbye' to so many dear friends we had come to know and love so deeply in the four-and-a-half years we were in Oxford. And, too, just having to say 'farewell' to Oxford—a place we truly came to call 'our' home—was heart-wrenching.
     But, in May, we returned to the USA.... Though it was *wonderful* to see our families and

have such a grand, sunny holiday on the farm, we were *so* homesick for England and found it a difficult cultural adjustment indeed. After such intense work on the thesis along with moving, we found ourselves mentally, physically, emotionally, and spiritually exhausted. But we had to call on strength somewhere deep in our beings to face the task of job-hunting during the summer. Many disappointments came when one New Testament teaching post after another was closed to Bob. Finally, the first part of August, the possibility of Bob pastoring a small church appeared on the horizon. Though it wasn't Bob's *choice* of occupations, it seemed a good place and way to re-enter American life again.... So life seemed to be 'settling down'; we were feeling stronger and more rested and we sensed a bit of inner peace *beginning* to grow in us about our return to America (though I'm certain our hearts will *for ever* be longing to be in two places at once).

Then, in the first part of October, I went to see a doctor to have several lumps checked in my left breast (which I'd had checked in Oxford just prior to our departure and was told they were only cysts). Subsequently I had a mammogram, which showed the lumps to be 'suspicious' enough to have biopsied. Still I was confident they were 'nothing'. Soon, the surgeon called Bob and me in to tell us they were cancerous. The next day my parents had to come and care for the boys and Bob and I were on our way to Mayo Clinic in Rochester, Minnesota (world renowned for the best possible medical care). There I had surgery to remove my left breast and lymph nodes. None of the remaining breast tissue nor any of the lymph nodes showed trace of cancer, so we are relieved and hopeful that the surgery itself eliminated the cancer.

However, in 3–4 months I will return to the clinic to have a preventive mastectomy on the right side as the type of cancer it was is highly likely to show up in the other breast at some time in the future. I will not need any chemotherapy or radiation treatments for which we are very, very thankful.

Why??? Why *us*? Why *now*? Why *anyone*? Why *ever*? And just when we were beginning to experience some semblance of happy ordered home life again. We'll doubtless *never* have those answers (at least in this earthly life), but *at this moment* Bob and I have found again that deep peace in Christ which *passes all understanding*.

I'm certain that Bob and I (individually and as a couple) have experienced nearly every emotion known to man during these past few weeks, at one time or another, and in varying degrees: hope, despair, disbelief, anger, fear, guilt, joy, sorrow.... Though we could see nothing clearly during the darkest moments of this experience—the future seemed veiled in a great, dark cloud —we knew *one* thing: that we couldn't face this experience alone. We needed the *tangible* expression of the Body of Christ in your prayers, flowers, phone calls, food, care for the boys, cards, letters, monetary assistance, words of peace, hope, and love—all expressions of love for us—to hold us up. And held up we have been. We have faced this thing with confidence and strength beyond our human understanding because you all have been strong for us.

As I look forward to the Thanksgiving and Christmas season, I feel very much emptied of any 'cheery' or 'traditional' phrases, 'appropriate' for the season, to put in this letter. I am solely consumed with thankfulness for *Life*—

and with humble praise for the Giver of Life, God in Christ Jesus.

> My soul magnifies the Lord,
> and my spirit rejoices in God my saviour,
> for he has regarded the low estate of his
>      handmaiden ... for he who is mighty has
>      done great things for me, and holy is his
>      name.
>
> (Luke 1:46–49 [RSV])

In His Great Mercy and Love,

Bob, Marge, Dan, Luke, Paul and Jacob.

I wouldn't like to think about the sort of letter *I* would have written to friends if I was in Bob and Marge's situation. I doubt if I'd have been so thankful or trusting. This is truly an example of keeping faith through the last half-hour. (I might add, too, that at the time of this writing, Marge has had both her breasts removed. Bob still feels ill-suited to his present post, but they are still holding fast to the Lord.)

No Christian is an island—Bob and Marge are good examples of how the Body of Christ may minister in practical ways when failure or severe trials come upon other members. For Christians to purposely ignore the pain and anguish of other believers is contrary to the message of the Bible. A personal relationship with Christ is a good thing, but if Christians refuse to get involved, then it is as James puts it,

> Are there still some among you who hold that 'only believing' is enough? ... Fool! When will you ever learn that 'believing' is useless without *doing* what God wants you to do? Faith that does not result in good deeds is not real faith.
>
> (James 2:19–20)

## Living In The Material World

The novelist Kurt Vonnegut recalls walking into a café some years back and above the cook's stove a sign read, 'If you're so smart, how come you ain't rich?' For him, this summed up all that is wrong with Western culture. In a society inured to conspicuous consumption, status symbols and outward appearances, we are judged by our possessions, our jobs, our accents, our educational background. The 'winners' receive the place of honour, while the 'losers' are turned away at the door. Therefore, the greatest threat to our personal equilibrium is failure.

In the film *Amadeus*, the story of the life of Mozart, the young Salieri dedicates his life to God through music. Salieri eventually becomes composer to the Austrian court; naturally he feels that his prayer has been answered by God. One day, however, the prodigy Mozart appears on the scene, eclipsing Salieri's mediocre competence. Hatred and jealousy possess Salieri's mind. This leads Salieri to renounce his faith in God and, according to Peter Shaffer's film version at least, Salieri destroys Mozart.

By the end of the film, Salieri is insane, and sees himself as a third-class messiah to the other crushed and depressed people of the asylum to whom he offers his worthless blessings. If nothing else, this scene captures the aversion—even the madness—associated with failure in a world which Vonnegut rightly claims places too high a premium on the outward appearances of success.

## We Do Not Have *All* The Answers

Why is God sufficient to maintain the faith of some Christians but not others when failure enters their lives? For example, why does King David have faith

to come before the Lord of Hosts as a convicted murderer and adulterer, asking for the forgiveness he
knows he will receive, when Saul falls on his sword instead of facing failure as a king? (See I Sam 31:1–5 and
II Sam 12:7–15.) Or why does Peter retain the faith to
know that Christ will forgive him for his great failing—his denial of Christ—not once, but three times,
while Judas condemned himself to death for his one
act of treason? I offer no sure answer to these questions. However, this I do know: Saul and Judas fell for
one of Satan's oldest ploys: self-judgement.

Both men set out to serve God. Both men achieved
some successes as well. Saul's early exploits against
the enemies of Israel made him seem a wise and fearless leader. In many ways he was. However, Saul liked
to do things *his* way and so ran afoul of God's mouth-
piece, the prophet Samuel. Secretly, Samuel anointed
another man, David, to be the King of Israel. When
Saul had found out, he became intensely jealous and
determined to kill David.

Even though Saul was now actively working against
God's will, he could have repented and stepped down
from his high position in humility, as Moses had done
when God indicated that it would be Joshua, not
Moses, who would lead the people into the Promised
Land. Instead, Saul continued to lead Israel until, in
his twentieth year as king, the Philistines once again
rose up to challenge Israel. Saul led a disastrous campaign and Israel was defeated on Mount Gilboa.

Overcome by his failure and, doubtless, overcome
by the news of the death of his own sons, Jonathan,
Abinidab and Malchishua, Saul, already grievously
wounded, begged his armour-bearer to kill him. This
he would not do. Again, at such a critical point, Saul
might have repented—accepting his defeat as his
punishment. Instead, Saul gave in to morbid

introspection and despair. Judging himself unredeemable—a fatal and tragic error for any human being to make—Saul tumbled forward on to the razor-sharp point of his sword and thus snuffed out his life.

Judas Iscariot had been a trusted member of Christ's inner circle of 12 and had the respectable task of looking after the money purse. Many people have depicted Judas in different ways. One popular view portrays him as a man acting out of noble motives: Judas, believing that Jesus was the Messiah, betrayed Christ to the authorities in order to prompt him to assume his role as political deliverer of Israel from the yoke of imperial Rome. In this scenario, our sympathies lie with Judas. He acted in good faith in betraying his master. Conversely, in all three synoptic Gospels, Judas is depicted as an outsider and traitor. John frankly calls Judas Iscariot a 'thief' and says he was 'possessed by the Devil'. This would suggest that Judas acted either out of jealousy or out of criminal intent and greed.

*Whatever* motivated Judas to act, he too could have resisted the temptation to pass final judgement on himself for the outcome of his betrayal. By turning Christ over to the Jewish authorities on that Thursday night in the Garden, he set off the events which led up to Christ's death by crucifixion—something I can't believe Judas had expected to happen.

Granted, once the plot to crucify Christ was a *fait accompli*, there was no brake to apply: Judas could not undo his mistake. Yet, hard as it would have been, he still might have repented. That Judas felt deep remorse for his actions is undeniable. Seeing Christ meekly submit to the rabid mob, rather than call down the heavenly hosts to begin the glorious revolution, Judas charged back to the Jewish high priests and cast the 30 pieces of silver on to the floor at their feet—which they very piously rejected, since their tradition taught that they could not accept 'blood money' for the temple coffers. Deeply dejected, Judas turned on his heel and fled into the night.

If ever there was a time when Satan confronted Judas it must have been now: 'See what you have done, Judas?' the Evil One might have whispered into the agitated man's ear. 'You've made a total wreck of your career as an apostle, and what's more, you've ruined the lives of all the other apostles who depended on you. And—worst of all, you scum—you've wasted the life of the good rabbi. No one will forgive you for all of this. You may as well go and kill yourself. The world will be better off without you!' Within the hour, Judas was dead by his own hand.

Satan's lies always prompt rash actions. Had Judas not given in to the urge to become his own judge and jury, he would have been wildly ecstatic in only three days when the empty tomb was discovered by the women on the first Easter Day.

Why is it that David and Peter found it possible to repent when they probably felt the alluring temptation to pass final judgement on themselves for their failures, while Saul and Judas could not bring themselves to cry out for forgiveness? I do not know. However, as Lewis' great lion, Aslan, says to the Pevensie children when they ask similar questions in the *Chronicles of Narnia* about the fate of other characters, 'That is a part of *their* story. It is of no consequence to *you*.'[7]

The apostle Paul puts it more diplomatically,

> ... we can see and understand only a little about God now, as if we were peering at his reflection in a poor mirror; but some day we are going to see him in his completeness, face to face. Now

all that I know is hazy and blurred, but then I
will see everything clearly, just as clearly as God
sees into my heart right now.        (I Cor 13:12)

### I've Made A Mess Of My Life

If you have failed at some important task, or if you
feel you have made a mess of your life and as a result
are contemplating suicide: don't do it. Wait. The
main reason you want to end it all is to be rid of the
bad feelings associated with failure. Satan would
dearly love you to act now—to take your life
immediately rather than seek other ways to resolve
your problems.

As I am a Christian, when I have failed and have felt
discouraged, I have benefited from close contact with
other believers whom I have trusted and respected.
Talk is not cheap—it is very therapeutic. If you are not
a Christian, you will still find many sympathetic listeners. The Samaritans are trained to listen and counsel—they may be contacted through the yellow pages
of your telephone directory. The DHSS are also prepared to counsel and advise. Christians aren't the only
ones who care about people!

Remember, whether you are a Christian or not,
God loves you and Satan hates you.

Love is patient and kind; love is not jealous or
boastful; it is not arrogant or rude. Love does
not insist on its own way; it is not irritable or resentful; it does not rejoice at wrong, but rejoices
in the right. Love bears all things, believes all
things, hopes all things, endures all things.
(I Cor 13:4–7 [RSV])

No matter how terribly you have failed, God understands and wants to heal you.

Hate, which is of the Devil, is the total opposite to love: hate is impatient and harsh; hate is jealous and boastful; it is arrogant and rude. Hate insists on its own way; it is irritable and resentful; it rejoices at wrong and recoils from right. Hate tolerates nothing, doubts everything, is pessimistic and endures nothing. Satan wants you to feel a humiliated and unloved failure. He wants you to pack it all in and commit suicide. Misery loves company.

This may be a wicked and sinful world, but love still remains—and always will. If this is so, then there is reason to go on living in the knowledge that, no matter how bleak and hopeless your situation may be, this, too, shall pass. As we saw in Judas' case, even postponing a planned suicide for a few days and talking it over with someone who can be objective about the problems in your life can make all the difference in how you perceive yourself.

Suicide does not solve problems. What lies beyond death? At least while you live, you may find ways to overcome your problems by seeking help. Once you have stepped into infinity, it is too late to go back.

Many opt for suicide as a means of finding everlasting peace, either in sweet sleep or in the comfort of unconscious oblivion. I doubt that death is like that. You may be taking your problems with you—and possibly finding that in eternity, there is no escaping from them.

My own experiences with failure have taught me one thing at least—nothing is irreparable. When I have plumbed the depths of despair—and many's the time I have—I have resisted the temptation to end it all. Now, looking back on the times when I very nearly did submit to Satan's urgings, I see that those odious days of pain have passed and the problems have either righted themselves or have been long forgotten.

### 'Not My Will But Thine, Abba, Father'

What is certain then? Notwithstanding the many biblical promises of victory and unending success (as seen in Psalm 1 and others), nowhere in the Bible is there a promise that any who have decided to follow God will be spared pain, suffering and failure. Indeed, often to be a Christian is more difficult than rejecting faith.

George Macdonald, who may be deemed an unsuccessful businessman and—to a large extent—a failed preacher, was so poor that he had to farm his children out to relatives, live apart from his wife and turn to writing books so that he could make ends meet. Rather than accusing God of being aloof while he endured the hardships of a failed career and being a failed family man, he reminds us that, 'The Son of God suffered unto the death, not that men might not suffer, but that their sufferings might be like his.'[8]

What *was* Christ's suffering like? How can we understand the intense pain? Elizabeth Goudge writes:

> Spiritual or physical agony (or mental) can be endured in silence only up to a point; beyond that point, if some sort of sound is not torn from the body, the mind cracks. It is typical of our Lord that whenever during his passion he reached this point, he did not groan, or cry out as sinners do, but prayed. Anyone who has ever tried, in the midst of any sort of pain, to turn from self to God, knows how hard it is to do, how the effort to do it seems to wrench one's whole being. Yet our Lord did it every time. He prayed ... 'Abba, Father, all things are possible unto thee; take away this cup from me: nevertheless, not what I will, but what thou wilt.'[9]

This is certain: each of us is destined to carry our

own cross—*carry* it, though, not *die* on it. Christ died on the cross once and for all. If we are to be, as Thomas à Kempis suggests, imitators of Christ, then when we face failure, pain, grief, anguish, shame or despair, we must turn from self to God and say, 'not my will, but yours, Father'. In doing this, we stand to lose all—but paradoxically, we also stand to gain all, though not necessarily in a material sense.

If this sounds too super-human, too spiritual, or—most importantly—just too hard, don't think Jesus found it easy, either. Goudge goes on to describe how Christ shrank from the dreaded ordeal of the humiliating failure and pain which lay before him in the Roman and Jewish courts. All of this pressed down hard on the mind and soul of the man, Jesus.

Still, in the selfless prayer, 'not my will, but thine' we have the unmitigated assurance that if we put our trust entirely into Christ's keeping—despite the failures we will encounter and the scars we must endure—whatever may happen to us, the best is yet to come. The theologian David Watson ends his poignant book *You are my God* by noting that his doctors had informed him that his once robust health had failed him.

> Having written these words, I heard only yesterday and unexpectedly, that I have to go into hospital in two days' time for a major abdominal operation which is expected to knock me out of action for the best part of six months. This has come as a total surprise, but I do know that the matter is both serious and urgent. I cannot say that I do not have any fears but I do know that 'trusting God in every situation' is a reality and no mere words.[10]

This illness was the beginning of the end of David

Watson. He died of cancer. But he died knowing that God calls us to live one day at a time, each day trusting in the sufficiency of the Father's love. And in this knowledge we may endure the pain of failure when it comes, and even benefit from it as well.

Just as the grapes first must be crushed, then violently fermented before excellent wine may be produced, so too must Christians expect to suffer in order to be transformed into light for a darkened world.

There are some who promise us that if we seek God, we may expect great blessings while the ungodly perish. Yes, the Christian may be compared to trees along a river-bank bearing luscious fruit each season without fail (as denoted in Psalm 1). Yet in the normal course of a year, along with the vitality of spring and the abundance of harvest, there must come the ravages of autumn and winter. And river or no river, the tree will shrivel and fail to produce fruit. In those times, we may take comfort in the words of Jesus Christ who says, 'My grace is sufficient for you, for my power is made perfect in weakness' (II Cor 12:9 [RSV]).

We who have roots in the West are infected with the double blight of pride and prosperity. The very suggestion that we be content with little or nothing runs contrary to the grain. Christ said, 'It is easier for a camel to go through the eye of a needle than for a rich man to enter the kingdom of God' (Luke 18:25). This does not imply that poverty is a prerequisite for eternal salvation. If it did, Joseph of Arimathea, described in the Gospels as 'a rich man', and Lydia who was in the lucrative purple-dye trade, would not be counted among the disciples who followed Jesus. A more accessible interpretation of Christ's words might be, 'It is easier for a camel to go through the eye of a needle than for a proud and self-sufficient person to enter the kingdom of God.'

## So Be It

Don't wait for a crisis or a great failure to ruin your equilibrium. Each one of us—rich or poor—is destined to make mistakes, to be victimised, to be failures from time to time. Putting our whole trust in God *right now*—no matter if we are currently riding high without any pressing cares, or if we are laid low in the throes of some great agony—this is the best way to accept our mistakes, hardships and failure and view them for their potential as blessings.

Shakespeare's sadder, though wiser, King Richard II puts it this way,

> Nor I, nor any man, that but man is,
> With nothing shall be pleas'd, till he be eas'd
> With being nothing.
> 
> (*Richard II* v. 5, 39–41.)[11]

On December 25th, 1747, John Wesley strongly encouraged Methodists to enter into a covenant with God through Jesus Christ. I invite you to read carefully, pray and meditate on Wesley's words. If you feel it is right for you, then I urge you to enter into this agreement with God:

> Put me to what you will, rank me with whom you will;
> Put me to doing, put me to suffering;
> Let me be employed for you or laid aside for you or brought low for you;
> Let me be full, let me be empty;
> Let me have all things, let me have nothing;
> I freely and whole-heartedly yield all things to your pleasure and disposal.
> And now, glorious and blessed God, Father, Son and Holy Spirit,
> You are mine and I am yours.

So be it.
And the covenant now made on earth, let it be
ratified in heaven. AMEN[12]

God calls us to enter into a relationship with him that
requires volitional participation on our part. Wesley's
words, 'put me to doing, put me to suffering' do not
mean we are inviting God to make us suffer; rather
they state that we desire, by the help of the Holy
Spirit, to be at God's disposal and to be used as he sees
fit in carrying out his purposes—knowing that, regardless of outward appearances, in all circumstances God
has our best interests at heart.

Of course, stoic submission to unpleasant circumstances only leads to bitterness and unhealthy anger.
God does not say in Psalm 46:10, 'Be numb and know
that I am God'; rather he says although all around you
are agitated, you may 'be still'; when your best efforts
seem to end in ignoble failure, 'rest assured'; when
everyone else has abandoned you, 'Lo, I am with you
always' (Matt 28:20 [RSV]): These are not cheap
words.

## Notes

[1]Corrie ten Boom, *Tramp for the Lord* (Hodder &
Stoughton Ltd: London, 1974), p 175.
[2]The idea of ceaseless praying is introduced by Paul
who writes, 'Always be joyful. Always keep on praying [pray without ceasing (RSV)]' (I Thess 5:16). JI
Packer writes, 'God ... [expects us to pray] before he
blesses our labours in order that we may constantly
learn afresh that we depend on God for [all things] ...
and so we shall know whom we ought to thank for
them' (JI Packer, *Evangelism and the Sovereignty of
God* [Inter Varsity Press: Downers Grove, IL, 1961],
pp 122–123). Another treatment of this admonition of

Paul's is found in the Russian classic *The Way of a Pilgrim* (RM French (trans), *The Way of a Pilgrim* [Philip Allan Publishers Ltd: London, 1931], p 7).

[3]Boom, *op cit*, pp 175–176.

[4]Alan P F Sell, 'Theology by Slogans', *One World*, no 119 (October 1986): p 18.

[5]James Brabazon, *Dorothy L Sayers: The Life of a Courageous Woman* (Victor Gollancz Ltd: London, 1981).

[6]Dorothy L Sayers, *The Man Born to be King* (Victor Gollancz Ltd: London, 1945), p 12.

[7]CS Lewis, *The Lion, the Witch & the Wardrobe* (Penguin: London, 1964).

[8]George Macdonald, *Unspoken Sermons. First Series*, quoted by CS Lewis in *The Problem of Pain* (Macmillan: New York, 1971), p 7.

[9]Elizabeth Goudge, *God So Loved the World* (Hodder & Stoughton Ltd: London, 1961), p 222.

[10]David Watson, *You Are My God* (Hodder & Stoughton Ltd: London, 1983), p 199.

[11]Shakespeare, *Complete Works* (Oxford University Press: Oxford, 1984), p 407.

[12]Copyright held by the Methodist Conference. Permission to publish by kind consent of the Methodist Publishing House.

# Epilogue

There is a fine line between despairing and finding satisfaction—even joy—when we suffer acute, or even slight, failure. If you have failed in some way, or if you know someone who has, the following points are some practical suggestions intended to turn your eyes off the self and fix them on others in the light of God's unmitigated love for all of us. By following these examples, you may become God's agent in helping to bring those who have failed back from the brink of despair.

1. **Get involved in people's lives.** In the words of John Donne, 'No man is an island' (*Devotions*, XVII).[1] During the lowest ebbs in my own life, I have seen Christ most clearly through the actions of others. Although it may be easier to turn our back on another's failures, the thing we *must* do is make ourselves available.

It doesn't take a special talent to invite someone who is going through a hard time into our home for a meal. By creating a non-threatening environment and by *listening*, we actually may participate in and aid a recovery of self-esteem, confidence and faith. Many times people say they wish they knew God's will for their lives. We all may be sure that part of the Lord's will is that we reach out and comfort the people who need our compassion and care.

When my wife and I first returned to the UK, we joined a church and settled down to the business of finding a place in the community. Although I knew finding work in Britain would be tough, I had no idea of what I was about to go through: I was unemployed for almost a year. As well as losing much of my confidence as a communicator, I began to feel paranoid—as if my being an American was keeping me from getting some of the jobs I had applied for.

Judith and I had spent most of our resources on daily living expenses. Yet, miraculously, each time we were down to our last few pounds, money dropped through our post-box, boxes of food were left on our doorstep, or we were invited out for meals. These were surely miracles as far as we are concerned, but the miracles were carried out by members of our church who were willing to be used by God and to extend God's love to us.

Anyone may become part of a miracle—if only they have a willingness to become involved in other people's lives. This involvement is not only our Christian duty—it is also the way Christ works in us.

2. **Don't wait for a crisis.** A Baptist minister friend of mine once said that too often he finds he only meets people when there is a problem. You will find it hard to offer much more than surface commiseration unless you have made the effort to meet people and make friends under less stressful circumstances. Then, should a crisis arise, you will be far better prepared to offer the right sort of assistance when and if it is needed. When Christ departed the earth after the Resurrection, he didn't say, 'Just call me if you need me'; instead he said firmly, 'I am with you always, even to the end of the world' (Matt 28:20). We must follow his example.

3. **Become a prayer partner.** Before leaving the United States to return to England, Judith and I approached 10 trusted friends in our church and asked them to pray for us daily. In return we promised to include them in our daily prayers. For nearly 2 years we kept these 10 people informed of our needs—and vice versa—through frequent letters. There were times when we really couldn't afford to send out 10 airmail letters, so often we consolidated our needs into 1

letter which was read out in a Sunday morning prayer group at our previous church back in Wheaton, Illinois. (I'm sure there were times when the events in our lives read like a soap opera!) Yet I am convinced that we were sustained largely owing to the prayers of these ordinary folk who said they would pray for us.

When someone has failed despite all of his best efforts, even if he has been praying regularly himself, make yourself available to pray with him or her. If it is impossible to meet, then offer to pray for that person on a daily basis. Two people praying is *always* better than one: 'I also tell you this—if two of you agree down here on earth concerning anything you ask for, my Father in heaven will do it for you (Matt 18:19). Better still, if a group of Christians pray, they may expect the Holy Spirit to guide their prayers in a way that will not go unheeded by the Father.

For prayer to be effective, it must be expectant (Mark 11:24). We must always pray in the certainty that God will indeed answer our petition. Beware, however. In the prayer given to us by Christ himself, 'The Lord's Prayer', Jesus teaches us to submit our will to that of God's: 'Thy will be done, on earth as it is in heaven' (Matt 6:10 [RSV]). After his agony in the Garden and his request, 'Father, if you are willing, please take away this cup of horror from me', Jesus goes on to add, 'But I want your will, not mine' (Luke 22:41–42). We must desire God's will rather than our own, often short-sighted, solutions.

Nevertheless, more good has been accomplished by earnest prayer than we shall ever know in this life. When we stand shoulder to shoulder with one of our brothers or sisters in need, committing ourselves to pray intensely for relief, then we are doing something positive and effective to help. Once again, on the eve of his crucifixion, Christ invited his closest friends to watch and pray with him in the Garden. Although the disciples let Christ down, the principle of having prayer partners is not lost on us, 2,000 years later.

Even if your prayers seem to go unheeded, never give up. Be persistent in your petition. Jesus' parables in Luke 11:5–8 and Luke 18:1–8 show us that sometimes answered prayer is delayed. This is not due to God's indifference, rather it is born of a love that always desires to develop and deepen a faith that is finally vindicated.

4. **Don't run away from adversity.** Many of us become depressed under pressure; we lose incentive and excitement about life. Soon we escape into our own introspective worlds to reduce emotional reactions to threats of pain or failure.

One of the best ways to adapt to the pain of failure is simply to accept it as normal. This book has tried to show it is an illusion to think we will never fail—I hope it has achieved this aim. We may not always succeed, but in God's economy we are *never* abandoned. He has a wonderful plan for each person who is willing to be used by him.

> 'For I know the plans I have for you,' says the Lord. 'They are plans for good and not for evil, to give you a future and a hope. In those days when you pray, I will listen. You will find me when you seek me, if you look for me in earnest'
> (Jer 29:11–13)

5. **Assume responsibility for your actions.** The Bible tells us that as we sow, so shall we reap. Scientists talk of cause and effect. The meaning is the same: if we are to be honest with ourselves and with God, we must be willing to admit to our own mistakes. If we can do this, the chances are we may begin to avoid repeating similar mistakes in the future.

6. **Draw upon your own failures as a means of counselling others.** One of the worst failures in my life came in 1981. Judith and I had become engaged and were living in Bristol. After planning an April wedding, we flew to the United States to visit my family, who had no idea I intended to get married. Some of the negative responses I got from the people at home undermined my confidence regarding the suitability of an Anglo-American marriage.

Adding to my doubts about getting married were financial problems. My job was to finish in July, and Judith's job was a temporary post. I began to wonder if we could afford to get married.

Three days before the wedding, my flat-mate presented me with a bill for our rates—my portion came to over £300. This meant the little money I had planned to use for a two-day honeymoon in Wales—and our first month's rent—was gone. In a blind panic, I rang Judith's parents and called off our wedding.

Many of my friends and family had flown over from the States and were already in England before they heard the bad news. For the next three months we were busy returning gifts and explaining that, while we were still in love, we weren't going to get married. What's more, Judith's parents still had to pay for the hall they had hired and were stuck with a big wedding cake and the caterers' bill.

You can imagine my anger when my flat-mate approached me gingerly a few days later and said he had made an error—that I actually owed him only £56! I was angrier still—but at myself—when our vicar had asked why I had agonised quietly for all these months when he was available to counsel Judith and myself. For most of my life, I had practised being quietly confident and a silent-suffering type. I saw that in effect my attitude was an inverse form of pride, which led to my failure.

As I have already quoted, 'no man is an island.' So, for the next few weeks Judith and I both sought help from Christians—some professional counsellors, some just sympathetic married couples—and in the end, we declared our love for one another in a very small but terribly romantic church service, miles away from Bristol.

Since then, my wife and I have had the opportunity to counsel an engaged couple who had second thoughts at the last moment. Living in an international city such as Oxford, we are also prepared to talk to Anglo-American couples trying to overcome a myriad of problems which face them after they get married.

People's past failures enable them to draw on their experiences and enable them to offer assistance to others. However, there are some instances where we meet problems too deep for us to handle. At these times, we should look to our churches for the numerous qualified people who, given half a chance, would be most willing to offer their services to a person in need.

7. **Don't put off until tomorrow what may be done today.** The time for action is *now*. If you belong to a church, go and see your minister, deacons or elders. Let them know you want to help others in need—or that you yourself have a problem. If you do not belong to a church, there are plenty of secular organisations that are in the business of caring.

If you believe that somebody ought to be doing something about the many problems that exist in this world, bear this Epilogue in mind—you probably are that somebody.

## Notes

[1]JM and MJ Cohen (eds), *The Penguin Dictionary of Quotations* (Penguin Books Ltd: Harmondsworth, 1986), p 144.

# Bibliography

Apichella, Michael A. 'Interview With a Rebel.' *The Christian Writer*. January 1985, p 24.

Armstrong, David. *A Road Too Wide*. Marshall Pickering: Basingstoke, 1985.

Attlee, Rosemary. 'A Mother's Story'. *Reader's Digest*. April 1984, p 115.

Billheimer, Paul E. *Destined For The Cross*. Tyndale House: Wheaton, IL, 1983.

Billingsly, Lloyd. 'I Preach Money.' *Eternity*. February 1986, pp 27–31.

Boom, Corrie ten. *Tramp for the Lord*. Hodder & Stoughton Ltd: London, 1974.

Boulding, Maria. *Gateway to Hope*. Fount: London, 1985.

Boykin, John. *Circumstances and the Role of God*. Zondervan: Michigan, USA, 1986.

Brabazon, James. *Dorothy L Sayers: The Life of a Courageous Woman*. Victor Gollancz Ltd: London, 1981.

Briscoe, Jill. *How to Fail Successfully*. Kingsway Publications Ltd: Eastbourne, 1983.

Camus, Albert. *The Plague*. Hamish Hamilton Ltd: London, 1948.

*Christian Praise*. The Tyndale Press: London, 1964.

Cohen, JM and MJ (eds). *The Penguin Dictionary of Quotations*. Penguin Books Ltd: Harmondsworth, 1986.

Colson, Charles. *Born Again*. Hodder & Stoughton Ltd: London, 1979.

Cruz, Nicky. *Satan On the Loose*. Oliphants: London, 1973.

Cumbers, Frank (ed). *The First Book of Daily Readings from the Works of Martyn Lloyd-Jones*. Epworth Press: London, 1970.

Cummings, Tony. 'How the Church was Lost.' *Buzz Magazine*. June 1985, pp 28–30.

Fellowes, Noel. *Killing Time*. Lion Publishing: Tring, London, 1986.

Fleming, James. *Personalities of the Old Testament*. Scribner's Sons, Ltd: London, 1951.

French, RM (trans). *The Way of a Pilgrim*. Philip Allan Publishers Ltd: London, 1931.

Gordon, Ernest. *Miracle on the River Kwai*. Tyndale House:

Wheaton, IL, 1984.

Goudge, Elizabeth. *God So Loved the World*. Hodder & Stoughton Ltd: London, 1961.

Greeley, Andrew M. *Confessions of a Parish Priest*. Simon & Schuster: New York, 1986.

Hare, Norman. 'Fresh Light on Bonhoeffer.' *Church Times*. September 19th, 1986, p 9.

Herriot, James. *All Things Bright and Beautiful*. Michael Joseph Ltd: London, 1976.

Hooper, Walter (ed). *CS Lewis Poems*. Geoffrey Bles: London, 1966.

Huggett, Joyce. *Conflict: Friend or Foe?* Kingsway Publications Ltd: Eastbourne, 1984.

*Hymns Ancient & Modern Revised*. William Clowes & Sons, Ltd: London.

'Irina Allowed to See Husband.' *Church Times*. August 15th, 1986, p 1.

'Irina to Stay in West for Time Being.' *Church Times*. December 26th, 1986, p 16.

James, Jo. *Don't Be Afraid*. Christian Literature Crusade: Fort Washington, PA, 1977.

Kilby, Clyde S and Lamp Mead, Marjorie (eds). *Brothers and Friends*. Harper & Row Publishers: Cambridge, Mass, 1982.

Lewis, CS. *The Great Divorce*. Fontana: London, 1971.

Lewis, CS. *The Last Battle*. The Bodley Head Ltd: London, 1956.

Lewis, CS. *The Lion, the Witch & the Wardrobe*. Penguin: London, 1964.

Lewis, CS. *The Screwtape Letters*. Geoffrey Bles: London, 1946.

Lyer, Pico. 'Hero in a Land of Few Heroes.' *Time*. June 30th, 1986, p 14.

Macdonald, George. *Unspoken Sermons. First Series,* quoted by CS Lewis in *The Problem of Pain*. Macmillan: New York, 1971.

Magnusson, Sally. *The Flying Scotsman*. Quartet Books Ltd: London, 1981.

'Many Visibly Moved As Revd David Armstrong Says Goodbye'. *Northern Constitution*. May 4th, 1985.

Marplan Survey commissioned by *Sunday Express*—reported in *Church Times*. December 12th, 1986, p 1.

Marshall, Catherine. *A Man Called Peter*. Fontana: London, 1964.

Marshall, Catherine. *The Helper*. Chosen Books: Waco, Texas, 1978.

Medina, Sara C. 'People.' *Time*. July 21st, 1986, p 21.

Nightingale, Rita. *Freed For Life.* Tyndale House: Wheaton, IL, 1984.

Packer, JI. *Knowing God.* Hodder & Stoughton Ltd: London, 1975.

Packer, JI. *Evangelism and the Sovereignty of God.* Inter Varsity Press: Downers Grove, IL, 1961.

Prior, David. *The Suffering and the Glory.* Hodder & Stoughton Ltd: London, 1985.

Reardon, Bernard MG. *From Coleridge to Gore: A Century of Religious Thought in Britain.* Longman Group Ltd: London, 1971.

Rice, Grantland. 'Alumnus Football.' *Werner's Readings and Recitations.* No 54 (1915), p 167.

'Russian Christians Reproach the West.' *Church Times.* August 29th, 1986, p 3.

Sayers, Dorothy L. *The Man Born to be King.* Victor Gollancz Ltd: London, 1945.

Scammell, Michael. *Solzhenitsyn.* Hutchinson & Co, Ltd: London, 1985.

Schaeffer, Francis. *The God Who is There.* Hodder & Stoughton Ltd: London, 1968.

Sell, Alan PF. 'Theology by Slogans.' *One World.* No 119 (October 1986), p 18.

Shakespeare, William. *Complete Works.* Oxford University Press: Oxford, 1984.

Swindoll, Patricia. 'Graham Offers Answers and Advice.' *Inform—Bulletin of Wheaton College.* Winter 1986.

Telford, John (ed). *Sayings and Portraits of Charles Wesley.* Epworth Press: London, 1927.

Tournier, Paul. *The Adventure of Living.* SCM Press Ltd: London, 1976.

Townsend, Anne J. *Suffering Without Pretending.* Ark Publishing: London, 1980.

Trapp, Maria Augusta. *The Trapp Family Singers.* Geoffrey Bles: London, 1954.

Trueblood, Elton. *The Humour of Christ.* Darton, Longman & Todd Ltd: London, 1965.

Vriezen, Theodore C. *An Outline of Old Testament Theology.* Blackwell & Mott: Oxford, 1958.

Watson, David. *You Are My God.* Hodder & Stoughton Ltd: London, 1983.

Weatherhead, Leslie D. *The Will of God.* Abingdon Press: Nashville, 1972.

Whyte, Alexander. *Bible Characters—The New Testament,* vol 2. Marshall, Morgan & Scott Publications Ltd: London, 1972.

## When Christians Doubt

Doubt is a taboo subject for many Christians. Doubt in oneself – and even more in others – can be a matter for anxious prayer. Yet doubt affects almost all of us at some point. It can be a growing time. It can lead to a firmer, more honest, more substantial faith.

Donald Bridge explores the varieties of doubt – unbelief, foolish doubt, faith under attack, doubt as a function of faith – and takes a hard look at such matters as the 'prosperity gospel' and unanswered prayer. Recognising that suffering both causes and results from doubt, he studies the experiences of Job and C.S. Lewis, and questions our approach to the Bible. He writes with compassion and a clear mind.

**When Christians Doubt** is for all of us who have encountered painful questions, but have been afraid to voice them aloud.

The Rev. Donald Bridge, a Baptist minister, is author of many books including **Spare the Rod and Spoil the Church**. He now lives in Stockton-on-Tees.

179pp                                                          £2.50